SANTA MUERTE AND THE MEXICAN DEATH CULT

Antonio Primavera

Codependent Heart Books
copyright © 2018 Antonio Primavera
First Edition: 31 October 2018All rights reserved under International
and Pan-American Copyright Conventions. Published in Mexico
and internationally by Codependent Heart Books.
ISBN: 2370000465924

For Sri Ganesha, La santisima muerte, my wife, and my mum.

Life will happen to you if you are ready to die. —Osho.

Preface

I figured I would get a few things said and out of the way before starting the book, give you, the reader, some backstory to how this book came to be. I have been a devotee of Santa Muerte from early 2007 to this day, a long while. Certainly nowhere near as long as a lot of *chilangos* (people from Mexico City) or *tepiteños* (people from Barrio Tepito), but probably longer than any other white foreigner. When I first met Santa Muerte in a *puesto* (market stall) near the Zócalo and Templo Mayor in Mexico City, I knew almost immediately that I would write a book about Her someday.

But it's not *just* a book about Her; it's about death and life and their inseparability. It is a story of living and dying, of watching others die, and coming to know and accept that *you* are dying every moment yourself. It is a love story, a story of finally "getting it."

In 2009 I began working as a volunteer psychotherapist at a low-cost mental health clinic in Barrio Tepito, Mexico's worst area as far as crime and violence. I was doing a practicum for my Masters and had to complete 500 hours of sessions with patients (The term *client* is not used in Mexico, as it has undesired business connotations.) While others in my program would never lower their selves to even going to Tepito, each of my 500 hours was gained at the clinic there. The volume was heavy. Think of doing triage or working in an emergency room. I often saw seven patients a day. Doing psychotherapy is not like other jobs where there is a lot of downtime. A psychotherapist has to be engaged and alert every moment of each fifty-minute session.

Many of my patients were devotees of Santa Muerte. A ten-year-old boy I worked with gave me a Santa Muerte painting as a gift for my services. The patients know that the therapists are not paid, so they sometimes give us gifts. Another man in his early twenties gave me a bone statue, about a foot high, of Santa Muerte. This statue became the centerpiece of my home altar or shrine.

Early on, I made visits to the original shrine in Calle Alfarería of Barrio Tepito. I made friends with Doña Queta, the woman responsible for the shrine, the first person to put a *capilla* (shrine) in the street (a practice that is very common with other saints) and found her very sweet and welcoming. Being recognized and hugged by her, and this seen by others, at the seventh annual Santa Muerte event in Ecatepec in 2009 probably saved my bacon. Ecatepec is a rough area, and the event was held under a train and highway overpass. Doña Queta and I are friendly acquaintances to this day. She let me interview her for this book, and she introduced me to other *participants* (That's the academic term for people I interviewed or spoke with while researching this thing.)

I wanted to write a PhD dissertation about Santa Muerte, but I knew that Harvard University, where I did my undergraduate degree in Literature and Creative Writing, would never have approved this research unless maybe I was doing a sociological or anthropological study. Psychology would not have allowed such a weird subject. After doing my Masters in Psychology, I had to seek out a place that was amenable to this subject and my approach to the research.

I found the Institute of Transpersonal Psychology in Palo Alto, California, which was the original and one of the only schools in the US offering PhDs in Transpersonal Psychology. ITP welcomed, nurtured, encouraged, and supported me in every way. I had so many great experiences at the biannual seminar retreats, held at an old monastery in the foothills of the Santa Cruz Mountains. Keynote speakers included the likes of Stanislav Grof, one of the founders of Transpersonal Psychology, Dean Radin, et al. I had wonderful professors such as, Rosemarie Anderson, Jay Dufrechou, John Elfers, Dorit Netzer, Kundan Singh, Gabriella Mihalache, Judy Schavrien, Mark McCaslin, Bahman Shirazi, et al.

The courses were interesting and engaging; they were experiential. Not only was the material transpersonal, but the instruction and atmosphere was as well. Each course incorporated actual *doing*, putting the theories into practice and learning from them. Classes were generally roundtable discussions where everyone learned from the others' experience. So many different ways of knowing and being, of living, were opened to me.

Much of this changed when a new president was brought in by the board of directors, a man so inept he had to look up *transpersonal* in the dictionary. He was won over after attending a transpersonal conference in Sofia, Bulgaria. Returning, he told us that he had been treated like a "rock star." He quickly renamed the school Sofia University and began turning the not-for-profit institute into a for-profit university with non-transpersonal course offerings and offering undergrad degrees, nearly-emptied ITP's coffers, fired a bunch of professors, and put the campus on lockdown with security guards barring entrance. This sounds like fiction. There were many occurrences and details to the story that I really don't feel like going into here. Fast forward…

The Institute of Transpersonal Psychology exists now only in name. It is gone. They fired all of the professors of note; the others resigned outright. Many students and professors went to the California Institute of Integral Studies in nearby San Francisco. When the new "Sofia University" saw the negative reaction of the public and the students, they paid some of the notables to be professors *emeritus* (meaning they do nothing; they do not give classes; their names merely appear in the school's propaganda.).

I hung in there, as I was at the dissertation writing phase and almost done. My committee were all great people. There was Jay Dufrechou as my doctoral chair (after Mark McCaslin was fired), John Elfers as my second chair, and Jonathan Young (who runs the Joseph Campbell Archive) as my third chair. But the new school harassed me to sign a new contract that had clauses like, if the school chooses to sue me I agree to pay the legal expenses and I agree to never sue the school. They also, without notice, cut off the pre-approved federal student loans of many, myself included. They pestered us to agree to some plan where we would pay them a ridiculous sum, which many of did not have, in order to finish our degrees. They said that if I did not sign the new contract and pay them, I would not receive the degree that I had worked on for around five years.

What was I to do? I decided to tell them to fuck off, that they were a bunch of lackeys and fakes. I decided to publish this book instead. That way, I could write the thing exactly as I wanted, I could do away with silly academic phrases like *lived experience* and *culture-sharing patterns*, and I could swear as much as I chose. To me, that sounded better than the other options to receive a degree from a school that isn't even recognized by the APA.

The university now calling itself Sofia University is a sham. It is a Chinese-owned front for espionage, an immigration scam/diploma mill complete with drone technology classes. It is no longer The Institute of Transpersonal Psychology. They bought the likes of Depak Chopra (the Oprah Winfrey of the transpersonal) to be their representative, their *bona fides* (as though anyone but flakey California New Agers believe him credible). That shows just how desperate and lost the school is now.

Anyway, enough of that. It hurt just to type the above because the school that I loved, the Institute of Transpersonal Psychology, meant a hell of a lot to me and to many others.

The bulk of the book, to me, the real meat, is the diary I kept during the project. For this reason, I have moved most of the dissertation academic bullshit to the appendix at the back of the book. This was suggested to me by my first Dissertation Chair Dr. Mark McCaslin. From the beginning, he always referred to the dissertation as my novel. Rather prophetic. But it was believed by my next Dissertation Chair, Dr. Jay Dufrechou that the school would never accept this format.

9

So, freed from the constraints of academia, I present a story that I believe is worth telling and I hope that you not only enjoy the read but are in some way transformed by it. Death comes to us all. When that happens, some of us will already be on a first-name basis with Her.

Chapter 1: Introduction

In recent years, as a psychotherapist working as a volunteer in a low-cost community mental health clinic in the notorious Barrio Tepito of Mexico City, and even before, on my first trip to Mexico City, I became acquainted with *Santa Muerte* (literally Saint Death), a Mexican folk saint who is the female personification of Death. She looks much like the Western image of the Grim Reaper: a skeleton wearing a monk's cowl and carrying a scythe. Santa Muerte might also be seen with an hour glass, balance scales, a globe of the earth, and an owl. As well, her robe can be in pretty much any color, even rainbow.

Image of Santa Muerte at shrine in Barrio Tepito, Mexico City, March 6, 2012.

While increasing numbers of devotees consider her a saint, the Roman Catholic Church vehemently disagrees and condemns devotion to her. The Roman Church says that death is not a saint; death contradicts their teachings of everlasting life in Heaven. At the same time, the majority of Santa Muerte's devotees consider themselves to be Catholic, and devotion rituals follow a Catholic form of novenas, rosaries, the mass, etc. Her altars typically have offerings of cigarettes, cigars, tequila or mezcal, flowers, water, apples, candy, marijuana joints, incense, candles, and money that reflect the likes and concerns of her devotees, and of course a statue of the saint, often wearing an elaborate dress (a wedding dress is not uncommon).

The early Christian writer Tertullian (2009) wrote the words, "Look behind you! Remember that you are but a man! Remember that you will die!" Supposedly the origin of this *memento mori* is that a Roman general's slave would say these things to his master, reminding him of his mortality, while he was being given a triumph after being victorious in battle—quite a departure from the current Western avoidance of the subject. *Mementos mori* are found commonly throughout Europe, and Mexico has its equivalents in the form of Day of the Dead celebrations, the nineteenth century *calavera* art of José Guadalupe Posada, and the like. The Day of the Dead and Santa Muerte both admit pre-Hispanic origins, as well as sharing the same November first holiday. Santa Muerte is seen by her Mexican devotees as related to Mictlantecuhtli, the Aztec god of death. For me, Santa Muerte is the perfect god of this world that is material, transient, and impermanent; she is a presence in our lives and an end to physical life on this plane, regardless of whatever may lie beyond it.

Gran fandango y francachela de todas las calaveras (Big Dance and Jamboree of all the Skeletons) (1910) by José Guadalupe Posada

Mexicans are close to death. Over sixty thousand people have died since the beginning of the drug war that President Calderón declared against the *narcos* in 2006 (making the casualties in both the Iraq and Afghanistan wars look like a mere trifle by comparison). *The Guardian* writes that "the story of the Calderón administration will pass into history as one that saw human rights violations, public insecurity, the military on the streets, more than 60,000 dead and 10,000 disappeared" (Hernández Navarro, 2012). These numbers have increased quite a bit since I began writing this book.

In Mexican Spanish, orgasms are colloquially called *muertes chiquitas* (little deaths). And this really says it all: life is richer because it ends, because of death. I and fellow devotees of Santa Muerte say that everyone meets death, but some of us will already be on a first-name basis with her. This seems to me akin to a type of behavioristic exposure therapy, whereby the fear of death is extinguished through repeated and progressive exposure to death.

Even without devotion to Santa Muerte, one living in Mexico sees graphic depictions of death every day in the newspapers. There are also Mexican notions of a good death, a holy death (*muerte santa*). Dying in an heroic fashion, such as by defending or providing for

14

one's family, or dying for a cause would be considered a good death. Even suicide, in some cases, is considered a good death. There is the legend of the young cadets (*Los niños héores*) who, rather than surrender to the Americans, draped themselves in the Mexican tricolor and threw themselves from the hill where sits Chapultepec Castle. While this story is generally known to be government propaganda, it demonstrates this notion of a good death.

Chapter 2: Literature Review

The purpose of this qualitative autoethnography is to explore the question: What are the patterns and divergences of the individual's experience of the practice of devotion to Santa Muerte in the lives of Her devotees in Mexico City?

In this literature review and as an introduction, I look at the history and origins of Santa Muerte, including the Aztec god and goddess of the underworld, Mictlantecuhtli and Mictecacíhuatl, and the various names by which Santa Muerte is known. I then address the practice of devotion to Santa Muerte, analyzing the significance of color, iconography, offerings, and ritual and prayer. Next, I present the two main centers of devotion in Mexico City, the church and the shrine, the condemnation of devotion to Santa Muerte by the Catholic Church, and the socioeconomic context for the practice of devotion to Santa Muerte. I conclude by presenting current representations and misrepresentations of Santa Muerte in the media. Again, the main portion of this book is my own research diary.

History and Origins of Santa Muerte

The exact origin of Santa Muerte is uncertain. In tracing the roots of devotion to Santa Muerte, there is no lack of debate. From academics, to the Roman Catholic Church, to the devotees themselves, emerge different versions of the origin story. Her name first appears in the records of the Spanish Inquisition in 1797 in a document titled *Concerning the Superstitions of Various Indians from the Town of San Luis de la Paz* (Chestnut, 2012).

Some researchers (Alvarado Gómez, 2004; Malvido, 2005; Flores Martos, 2008; Perdigón Castañeda, 2008) believe that Santa Muerte has her origins in the image of the European Grim Reaper, *La Parca* in Spanish, which was brought to Mexico by the Spanish at the time that the plague was ravaging their homeland in the 16th century. As images such as the Grim Reaper and the *danse macabre*, expressing the universality of death, were common in medieval Europe at that time (Clark, 1950), their connection to Santa Muerte is convincing.

The Dance of Death (1493) by Michael Wolgemut

Malvido (2005) writes that, during times of plague and epidemic, people often offered devotions to skeletal figures, which were at times associated with miraculous cures, making connections between Santa Muerte's popularity in the current state of modern Mexico unavoidable.

Such traditions may have spread to the Americas through the cult of the Spanish canonical Saint Pascual Bailón, popularly venerated in the state of Chiapas in southern Mexico and in parts of Guatemala as San Pascualito Rey (*-ito* is a diminutive ending, a topic to which we will return in the *Names* section of this book; *rey* means *king*).

Bailón was a Spanish Franciscan friar who lived from 17 May 1540 to 17 May 1592, never visited the Americas, and was not canonized until 1690. Yet, he is reported to have appeared in visions to a Mayan man in Guatemala which was, at the time, along with

Mexico, part of the Viceroyalty of New Spain, during a plague in the 1650s, which the saint was credited with ending. He became known as *el protector de los indios* (the protector of the Indians). His image is venerated in the form of a crowned skeleton (Navarrete Cáceres,1982; Feldman, 1999; Alvarado Gómez, 2004; Chestnut, 2012; Quezada, 1979, 1985).

As to the devotees themselves, it seems that most, if not all, believe that Santa Muerte is, or is related to, the pre-Hispanic Aztec lord and lady of the underworld Mictlantecuhtli and Mictecacíhuatl who I will address later (González Olivo, 2009; Velázquez, 2009; Chestnut, 2012).

Anthropologist Katia Castaneda Perdigón (2008) argues vehemently that the history of the current concept of death and its iconography, reflected in the Santa Muerte of this century, relates more to the Judeo-Christian-Islamic religion than with "the unwritten voice of the pre-Hispanic peoples" (So, if it's unwritten, you can say whatever the hell you want and who can argue?). It was part of the essential elements of Catholic dogma, which was introduced in the colonial icon *Triumph of Death* (Castaneda Perdigón, 2008). While Castaneda Perdigón urges tolerance and acceptance of Santa Muerte and Her devotees, she says that any alleged connection between the saint and indigenous spirituality is a "lie," (Instituto Nacional de Antropología e Historia, 2008; Castellanos, 2004). While Castaneda Perdigón's scholarship is interesting, even impressive, I think it is more important, and respectful, to listen to what Santa Muerte's devotees believe about the saint themselves.

The Triumph of Death (1562) by Pieter Bruegel the Elder

Regardless of how veneration of Santa Muerte may have originated, the cult has become a major phenomenon only recently. (NB: The word *cult* carries a negative connotation in American English that it does not in the Spanish equivalent *culto* translated here.)

According to Sra. Tamez, a devotee from Monterrey, Nuevo León, her grandmother was a Santa Muerte devotee, suggesting that the cult has been around since the mid-20th century (Sevigny, 2002). The cult is said to have spread since the mid-1960s, and its modern version is widely considered, especially by devotees, to have first appeared in the state of Hidalgo, north of Mexico City, around 1965 (*Culto a la Santa Muerte*, n.d.; *Los poderosos secretos*, n.d.; *Santa Muerte: Novena e historia de su culto*, n.d.; *Solucione sus problemas con la Santa Muerte*, n.d.; Uribe Ordaz, n.d.; Johnson, 2004; Fragoso Lugo, 2007; Guttman, 2007; Instituto Nacional de Antropología e Historia, 2008; González Olivo, 2009; Velázquez, 2009). The cult has also established roots in the states of Mexico, Guerrero, Veracruz, Tamaulipas, Campeche, Morelos, Nuevo León, Chihuahua, and the Federal District, especially

Barrio Tepito (Galindo García & Galindo Flores, 2006;Flores Martos, 2007; Ferrer, 2008; *Culto a la Santa Muerte*, n.d.).

The different versions of the origin of practice of devotion to Santa Muerte are interesting, because what the devotees believe about their cult's history is in many ways more interesting than what its true origin may be. It's like the psychological effects of *placebo* and *nocebo*; whether or not it works depends or whether or not you *think* it will work.

There are also some common themes. The cult is associated with indigenous peoples, and there is a melding of Catholic and pagan beliefs (more on the pagan nature of Catholicism to follow). Furthermore, the cult is most often associated with marginalized populations of Mexican society, including the poor, indigenous peoples, homosexuals, prostitutes, transgender, and criminals. The exact origin of Santa Muerte remains a mystery but likely predates Christianity, several researchers have said (Baez-Jorge, 1998; Araujo Peña, Barbosa Ramírez, Galván Falcón, García Ortiz, Uribe Ordaz, n.d.).

John Thompson (1998) of the University of Arizona's Southwest Center has found references to Santa Muerte dating to 18th Century Mexico. According to one account, indigenous people tied up a skeletal figure and threatened it with lashings if it didn't perform miracles or grant their wishes; a similar tale is recounted by Sir John Woodroffe (2009) as relates to San Antonio (Saint Anthony, my namesake). One source traces the legend to Veracruz, where a sorcerer claimed to have seen an image of Death in his dreams. The apparition ordered him to create a likeness of Her, promising all devotees a painless death (Navarrete Cáceres, 1982). Other accounts from the 20th Century find Santa Muerte linked to love potions and used with prayers to attract a romantic interest (Chestnut, 2012), which, as we will see later, is an area where Santa Muerte has much influence.

Santa Muerte stems partly from a long-standing religious and cultural tradition in Mexico of seeing death as part of life (Matovina, 2002). During Day of the Dead celebrations, for example, hundreds, if not thousands, flock to cemeteries to sing, pray, and sit vigil for deceased friends and family members. Children partake in the festivities by eating skulls formed of chocolate or sugar. Matovina (2002) also notes that the Aztecs were known to hold month long celebrations for the dead. Eventually, that indigenous tradition melded with the Catholic ritual of praying for souls in purgatory.

Mictlantecuhtli and Mictecacíhuatl: Lord and Lady of the Aztec Underworld

Little has been written about Mictlantecuhtli (Lord of *Mictlan*), the Aztec lord of the underworld (*Mictlan*), and virtually nothing about his partner, wife, consort, or female half Mictecacíhuatl. What is known today of this deity is related to his part in the myths of other, more popular, deities such as Quetzalcoatl (the plumed serpent).

Statue of Mictlantecuhtli in Museo de Templo Mayor, Mexico City

Statue of Mictlantecuhtli in Museo de Antropología, Xalapa, Mexico.

As lord of Mictlan, the lowest and northernmost level of the Aztec underworld (*inframundo*) or world of the dead, Mictlantecuhtli and his consort are said to live in a windowless house (Smith, Wharton & Olson, 2003; Miller & Taube, 2003). He is depicted as a blood-spattered skeleton with eyeballs in the sockets, his tongue protruding, and usually wearing a necklace of human eyeballs, in many ways quite similar to the depictions of the Hindu deity Kali. He is associated with owls, bats, and spiders (Fernández, 1996). In statues excavated at the Templo Mayor of Tenochtitlán (the center of present day Mexico City) his arms are outstretched in a menacing fashion, supposedly with the threat of ripping apart the dead (Matos Moctezuma & Solis Olguín, 2002). "In the Aztec world, skeletal imagery was a symbol of fertility, health, and abundance, alluding to the close symbolic links between death and life" (Smith, Wharton & Olson, 2003).

Image of Mictlantecuhtli in church courtyard, San Ándres, Mixquic, Mexico City.

Pile of skulls and bones below image of Mictlantecuhtli in church yard, San Ándres, Mixquic, Mexico City.

In Aztec mythology, the dead are guided through Mictlan by the psychopomp *itzcuintli* (medium-size, gray, mostly hairless Mexican dogs that are featured in the zoo of Mexico City) where they are subjects of Mictlantecuhtli. Mictlantecuhtli rules over each of the three types of the dead (i.e., those who died normal deaths, by old age, disease, etc.; those who died heroic deaths, such as in battle, by sacrifice, or during childbirth; and non-heroic deaths, such as suicide) (Matos Moctezuma & Solis Olguín, 2002).

While human sacrifice and ritual cannibalism were practiced by the Aztecs, there seems to be no hard evidence that these practices were specifically associated with Mictlantecuhtli.

The Aztec myth most associated with Mictlantecuhtli is that of the story of the creation of the world, where Quetzalcoatl descends to Mictlan to steal the bones of a previous generation of gods.

Mictlantecuhtli tries to stop Quetzalcoatl from taking the bones. Quetzalcoatl escapes with the bones but, in the process, drops and breaks them. These bones were then used to create the various races of humans (Miller & Taube, 2003; Read & González, 2000).

The Names

Most Mexican names have nickname counterparts, though I have yet to find any Mexican who knows a name for this phenomenon. Whether or not these nicknames are related rationally to the official name, they are typically in diminutive form as the diminutive form carries a sense of familiarity. Some examples: Jesús is *Chucho* or *Chuy*, Guadalupe is *My wife* or *Lupe*, Guillermo is *Memo*, Francisco is *Pancho*, and Ignacio is *Nacho*.

With few exceptions anything in Mexican Spanish can be made smaller to make it nicer and more familiar, including divinities. The canonical saint, San Judas Tadeo (Saint Jude) (patron saint of lost and desperate causes), is called, familiarly, *San Juditas* in Mexico.

As well, Santa Muerte has a number of such nicknames. One of the most common is *Santísima Muerte* (Holiest or Most Holy Death). Other of Santa Muerte's sobriquets include *La Flaquita* (The Skinny Girl), *La Huesuda* (The Bony Lady), *La Madrina* (The Godmother), *La Hermana Blanca* (The White Sister), *La Niña Hermosa* (The Beautiful Girl), *La Señora Poderosa* (The Powerful Lady) (Chestnut, 2012), *La Niña Bonita* (The Pretty Girl), *La Niña Blanca* (The White Girl) (Galindo García & Galindo Flores, 2006), *LaSeñora de las Sombras* (The Lady of the Shadows), *La Parca* (The Spanish Grim Reaper) (González Olivo, 2009).

These sobriquets show the degree orf closeness to the saint that her devotees feel towards Her. As with calling San Judas Tadeo, San Juditas, the diminutive form creates or demonstrates closeness. But devotees of Santa Muerte will, at times, also call her *cabrona* (literally *big she-goat*, or *bitch*), terms that they would not use for a canonical saint (Chestnut, 2012).

Santa Muerte is female. This is not solely because 'muerte' is feminine is Spanish. There is an Argentine folk saint called San La Muerte, which is masculine as shown by the *'san'* honorific. It is notable that Santa Muerte is a female figure and this is in itself an innovation, as previously death had no specific gender representation (Lamas, 2002). Mexico is a country where Marian worship is very noticeable, prevalent, and Santa Muerte is carefully dressed in a garment reminiscent of the virgins of the altars, or even the funeral ornamentation of deceased crowned nuns from the colonial era (Lagarriga Attias, 1975; Ortiz Ehaniz, 1990; Granziera, 2004). The images of Santa Muerte receive the treatment that is given to images of patron saints and virgins in popular Catholicism; they are treated as if they were real people who give favors in return for the faith of the believer. (Garma, 2009).

The Practice of Devotion

I think it important here to look at devotional and magical practices associated with Santa Muerte. The practice of devotion to Santa Muerte touches on each of the three of Stanislav Grof's "three major regions of transpersonal experience" (i.e., "experiences such as identification with other people or groups, encounters with mythical-archetypal figures, and magic") (Daniels, 2005).

Elaborating, I see that devotees of Santa Muerte feel affinity, respect, and watch over other fellow devotees in ways that are seen much less in connection with canonical saints; my own treatment as a white foreigner attending masses in typically dangerous Barrio Tepito attests to this. Seldom have I been greeted more warmly or felt more welcome than at a Santa Muerte event in Barrio Tepito. Santa Muerte *is* Death; there are few more explicit mythical-archetypal figures than

Death. Practice of devotion to Santa Muerte involves the practice of magic, whether by the devotee or by the shaman (*chaman/curandero*) whose services are sought by respectful non-devotees.

Devotion

Much of devotional practice to Santa Muerte takes the form of Roman Catholic devotional practices, which are considered a gift of oneself, or one's activities, to God. Devotion means a willingness and desire to dedicate oneself to serve God, either in terms of prayers or in terms of a set of pious acts such as the adoration of God, and the veneration of the saints or manifestations of the Virgin (Thurston, 1911; Carroll, 1989).

Roman Catholic devotions are "external practices of piety" which are not part of the official liturgy of the Catholic Church but are part of the popular spiritual practices of Catholics (Santi, 1910; Ball, 2003).

Catholic devotions do not become part of liturgical worship, even if they are performed within a Catholic church, in a group of Catholics, or in the presence of a priest (Dues, 1992). Devotion to saints, with the Virgin Mary as the most prominent example, is a key characteristic of Roman Catholicism (Ball, 2003). Catholic devotions have various forms, ranging from formalized, multi-day prayers such as novenas (Ball, 2003) to activities which do not involve prayers, such as Eucharistic adoration outside Mass, visiting shrines, the wearing of scapulars (Santi, 1910), lighting candles and incense, the veneration of the saints, and even horticultural practices such as maintaining a Mary garden (Ball, 2003).

Common examples of Catholic devotions include the Rosary, the Stations of the Cross, the Sacred Heart of Jesus, the Holy Face of Jesus, the various scapulars, the Immaculate Heart of Mary, Our Lady of Guadalupe, Seven Sorrows of Mary, novenas to various saints, pilgrimages and devotions to the Blessed Sacrament, and the veneration of saintly images, etc. All of the above examples fit together well with the practice of devotion to Santa Muerte.

In Catholicism, and Latin American Catholicism more specifically, the concept of the folk saint is widespread and common. These folk saints are popular locally, and can be both canonical, as is the case with San Simón or Maximón, or non-canonical, as with Jesús Malverde (Arriola, 2003; Griffith, 2003) or Santa Muerte (Mendelson, 1965; Pieper, 2002). What makes Santa Muerte unique, then, as a folk saint is that She was never a living person, but is instead a supernatural being, maybe the archetype par excellence.

So much of the history of the development of Catholicism has involved the absorption of local "pagan" spiritual traditions that it is difficult to speak of any Catholicism without saying something about its syncretic nature.

In Bernal Diaz del Castillo's *The Conquest of New Spain* (1963), the author, a former conquistador with Hernán Cortés, recounts his band's meeting with the Aztec priests. He describes the priests' long, black locks of hair as being matted together with dried blood from ritual human sacrifices. After a short explanation of the Catholic faith by their conquerors, the Aztec priests were cleaned up and their hair cut. They were baptized and declared priests of Christ, Catholic Priests. Such hasty conversions, lacking Europe's 1500 years of assimilation to this imported faith or belief system, were bound to lead to the syncretism that we see in Mexico today.

Mexican spirituality at the time of the Spanish Conquest was polytheistic, pantheistic, and animistic. "Thus, pre-Hispanic Mexican and Central American images were understood to actually take on the character and spirit of the deities they represented, a perspective that was considered idolatry by European Catholics.

As the inheritors of this tradition, folk saints of the region often are seen to act directly in the lives of their devotees rather than serving as mere intermediaries (like Catholic priests), and they are themselves venerated. Visitors frequently treat the representations of folk saints as real people, observing proper etiquette for speaking to a socially superior person or to a friend depending on the spirit's disposition—shaking hands, or offering it a cigarette or a drink" (Graziano, 2006).

This describes well the attitude of the devotee to Santa Muerte. A familiarity exists between Saint and devotee that is seen less in devotion to canonical saints. Canonical saints serve as a bridge to the divine, while folk saints work directly in the lives of their devotees.

For the devotee of Santa Muerte, there is a greater proximity, a greater closeness than is typically felt by devotees to canonical saints, and for this reason the devotee needs no intercessor, as is the rule in Catholicism. Interaction between devotee and the divinity is immediate rather than mediated. "In pre-Columbian Mesoamerican tradition, representation meant embodiment of these holy figures rather than mere resemblance, as it did in Europe" (Parkinson Zamora, 2006). Much as in other primordial traditions, such as Hindu, the image of the divine is not a symbol of the divine, but is itself divine (Woodroffe, 2009) (e.g., a statue of Santa Muerte *is* Santa Muerte).

The figures of the saints, virgins, and other characters represent Jesus Christ as having existed historically. However, in Mesoamerican religions, death can be a deity and outside of human time or existing since primordial time. For example, Mictlantecuhtli was the Aztec deity of death and of the underworld. Many believers in Santa Muerte highlight this relationship, arguing that the cult has pre-Hispanic roots.

This syncretism contains more elements. The iconographic representation of death as a skeleton with a scythe is seen often in medieval paintings as a symbol of human mortality and the illusions of earthly/temporal life. Painters like Cranach and Brueghel, as well as Posada in Mexico, highlight this representation. In Spanish-speaking America the skeleton serves to remind of the need for a good death, a *muerte santa*, that a believer dies having repented of his sins and having confessed (Garma, 2009).

The Significance of Color

Color plays an important role in the practice of devotion to Santa Muerte; so much so that R. Andrew Chestnut, in his 2012 book, the first serious critical study of this topic in English, *Devoted to Death: Santa Muerte, the Skeleton Saint*, titles his chapters with the various colors of her devotional candles, colors which my participant-devotees say are meaningless. Maybe that professor should learn some Spanish.

When Santa Muerte statues are dressed in particular colors, they represent certain powers or attributes. Equally, the color of the candles used in magical ceremonies corresponds to a desired result.

Blue is for wisdom, students, and teaching (Velázquez, 2009); for study and concentration (González Olivo, 2009); spiritual understanding, kindness, and happiness (*Solucione sus problemas con la Santa Muerte*, n.d.).

Black is for total protection, and especially for protection against magic used against oneself (Galindo García & Galindo Flores, 2006); against *brujería* (black magic), against works of Santería, Palo Mayombe, or voodoo (Velázquez, 2009); for invoking negative energies (González Olivo, 2009); for force and power (*Solucione sus problemas con la Santa Muerte*, n.d.); to rid oneself of negative influences in the family, business, or work (*Santa Muerte: Novena e historia de su culto*, n.d.).

Gold is for economic power, success, money, thanks to Santa Muerte and beginning of worship, and for business (Galindo García & Galindo Flores, 2006); for opening doors/removing obstacles (González Olivo, 2009); for the work of initiation and understanding (*Solucione sus problemas con la Santa Muerte*, n.d.).

Bone is for maintaining peace, harmony, and for success (Galindo García & Galindo Flores, 2006). Red represents love, passion, harmony with your partner and the people around you, and for emotional stability (Galindo García & Galindo Flores, 2006); it is the primordial color for whatever ritual related the sentimental (González Olivo, 2009).

Purple helps to attract health and counteract all sickness, whether natural or provoked (González Olivo, 2009); to open doors to the supernatural and the divine (*Solucione sus problemas con la Santa Muerte*, n.d.).

White is for purification; it clears away negative energy, envy, and rancor among family members (Galindo García & Galindo Flores, 2006); to purify desire (González Olivo, 2009); to request protection, health, and money (*Solucione sus problemas con la Santa Muerte*, n.d.); to eliminate negative vibrations in the family (*Santa Muerte: Novena e historia de su culto*, n.d.).

Green is used for legal problems (Galindo García & Galindo Flores, 2006); for justice and lawyers, and for healing (Velázquez, 2009); to maintain unity with loved ones (*Solucione sus problemas con la Santa Muerte*, n.d.); for peace, family harmony, union, and progress (*Santa Muerte: Novena e historia de su culto*, n.d.).

Amber is used against the sickness of drug addiction and alcoholism (Galindo García & Galindo Flores, 2006).

The color pink is also used for love-related rituals (González Olivo, 2009).

Brown is used for calling the spirits from the beyond (*la más allá*) (*Solucione sus problemas con la Santa Muerte*, n.d.).

Yellow is used to attract wisdom and luck (*Solucione sus problemas con la Santa Muerte*, n.d.).

Considering that the meanings ascribed to the colors overlap and, at times, contradict one another, it should be no surprise that the same is found in other spiritual traditions (Sunrise, 1998; Yronwode, 1995a).

Iconography

Images of Santa Muerte contain various attributes that contribute to a significant iconography. Like the Grim Reaper, She is typically pictured holding a scythe. As understood among believers, the symbolism of the scythe represents a double aspect: as a weapon, to cut the negative energy of enemies so as to eliminate its effect, and as a cultivation tool, that represents the harvest of new hope and future prosperity (Ambrosio, 2003; González Olivo, 2009; Velázquez, 2009).

The globe that She often holds represents the material/physical world of form "which is a tomb, considering that resurrection is a birth beyond the terrestrial plane" (Velázquez, 2009). Authors have reported that the globe She holds in her hand represents her total power, and that, with Her, one is assured success in whatever undertaking, as well as confidence, leadership, conquests, and independence (Ambrosio, 2003; González Olivo, 2009; Velázquez, 2009).

The balance scale, said to be of Chaldean origin, is a mystical symbol of justice balanced between punishment and guilt, that Santa Muerte is a just judge, and that She insures stability, peace, firmness, and security (Ambrosio, 2003; González Olivo, 2009; Velázquez, 2009).

The writers, in describing the hourglass, mention Cronos, the Greek god of time, the passing sand symbolizing the time of one's life. As well, they say that the hourglass symbolizes the relationship between the superior and inferior worlds, related to the perpetual movement of magical and divine beings. The hourglass urges one to have patience, and Santa Muerte will help one to attain every goal in life (Ambrosio, 2003; González Olivo, 2009; Velázquez, 2009).

The owl with which Santa Muerte is often pictured is said to be a nocturnal bird that can easily see in the dark and, having an infallible sense of orientation, represents one's eyes and feelings. The owl is at one's side to help in situations of blindness and confusion. The owl is a symbol of wisdom. As a companion of Santa Muerte, the owl acts as a messenger, and one can ask favors of the owl. In general, the owl helps one to increase intelligence, knowledge, ideas, and orientation (Ambrosio, 2003; González Olivo, 2009; Velázquez, 2009). As we have seen earlier, the owl is also associated with Mictlantecuhtli and with death.

The lamp is a symbol of intelligence and the spirit. Its light helps to irradiate the way and the decisions one must make in life. Its light never extinguishes, and is always there to give light in times of darkness, and to show the truth where there is ignorance. In general terms, the lamp helps one to see with clarity, to have spiritual peace, and to live in harmony (Ambrosio, 2003; González Olivo, 2009; Velázquez, 2009).

The tunic or cowl that Santa Muerte wears covers her from head to toe, representing the way that one hides their true self from others. As she is a skeleton covered by her tunic, so are humans covered by their flesh which hides the fact that they are all the same underneath; it is difficult to distinguish the bare skull of a friend or a neighbor form that of an enemy (Ambrosio, 2003; González Olivo, 2009; Velázquez, 2009). This speaks again to the notions of equality associated with Santa Muerte.

Offerings

Santa Muerte devotees attend to their practice by lighting candles and making offerings, reciting prayers, often in the hope of receiving favors. These offerings generally draw upon Catholic symbolism or forms, but are also mixed with elements of indigenous spirituality. There are traditions about what sorts of offerings are appropriate to Santa Muerte.

A wide range of other devotional practices can be found among Catholics. An example is the use of a home altar. This practice dates back to the early Christians who used to pray in their homes before churches were built for public worship, or during times of persecution. In a home altar, a cross usually hangs on the wall, and images of Jesus, the Blessed Virgin, and saints may be displayed, along with a copy of the Bible or other devotional literature (Storey, 2007).

The ritual books of Santa Muerte contain instructions for setting up an altar or shrine for the practice of devotion in the home, office, or other locations. As well, the books describe what sort of accoutrements and offerings should accompany the altar. Central to any shrine is the image, which can be in the form of a statue or a picture. The altar must also be consecrated; the instructions vary and are quite detailed, and the time of day that this is done corresponds to different spiritual forces.

In the morning, Santa Muerte is said to be filled with the powerful vibrations of the waking sun, with entrepreneurship, and ready to meet challenges. In the midday sun she is at the height of her power, and at night she manifests the energy of the dark forces (Velázquez, 2009). Another book says that her image must face west, where "the last rays of the sun's light fall, die, and herald the kingdom of the night" (*Solucione sus problemas con la Santa Muerte*, n.d.).

The various offerings to Santa Muerte that are placed on the altar include bread, water, fruit, incense, sweets, flowers, cigarettes and cigars, and wine and alcohol (Figueroa, 2006; *Culto a la Santa Muerte*, n.d.; *Solucione sus problemas con la Santa Muerte*, n.d).

Impromptu Santa Muerte street altar in Calle Alfarería,
Barrio Tepito, Mexico City, November 1, 2011.

Bread should never be omitted from the altar. Bread insures that neither Santa Muerte nor the devotee ever go hungry. Bread is indispensable for communication with her. The bread should be replaced twice-weekly, and when it is discarded it should not be placed in the trash, but under a tree where its energy can be rechanneled (*Culto a la Santa Muerte*, n.d.).

Water is another offering that must always be placed on the altar, preferably in clear glass. The water must always be clean and changed often. The water has both spiritual and material aspects; it helps to purify and to channel energy. According to *Solucione sus problemas con la Santa Muerte* (n.d.), Santa Muerte's preference is for tap water. The book *Culto a la Santa Muerte* (n.d.) urges the devotee to observe the water for the following conditions and their meanings. Cloudy water means problems with family members or with others, and should be changed soon. Water with little bubbles means that spiritual and/or economic tranquility will soon be realized. Water that is clear and clean for a long time means that it is a suitable time to petition Santa Muerte with good results and good energy.

Fruit is considered an apt tribute to Santa Muerte; whatever type of fruit is said to remove envy and bad energy. The fruit should be consumed by the devotee the following days, and should never be thrown in the trash. *Solucione sus problemas con la Santa Muerte* (n.d.) says that red apples have the power to capture negative energy, while *Culto a la Santa Muerte* (n.d.) says that they insure that Santa Muerte will answer one's requests. This book also says that yellow apples insure that the devotee never lacks money or prosperity.

Solucione sus problemas con la Santa Muerte (n.d.) says that incense should be burned a couple of times a week, and that the type does not matter, while *Culto a la Santa Muerte* (n.d.) gives specific functions for the various types following. Copal changes negative energy into positive energy, and is good for opening a business. Sandalwood attracts success, abundance, and prosperity. Myrrh removes envy, intrigues, and hatred. Rose attracts love and passion; it is an aphrodisiac that awakens sexual desire. Jasmine "cures" a business; it attracts clients and cleans bad vibes. Musk eliminates sickness and opens the way to health; it purifies the environment and keeps anything bad from happening to the devotee.

Santa Muerte has a sweet tooth, and among her favorite offerings is candy. She likes all sweets, lollipops, hard candy, bonbons, etc., but her favorite is chocolate which is said to get rid of bad vibes and envy (*Culto a la Santa Muerte*, n.d.). Chocolate is also indigenous to Mexico. Honey is also recommended for its purity (*Solucione sus problemas con la Santa Muerte*, n.d.). The book, *Culto a la Santa Muerte* (n.d.) says that the sweets need be natural in order to permit the flow of vital energy.

Flowers are also among favorite offerings to Santa Muerte. *Culto a la Santa Muerte* (n.d.) recommends roses, gardenias, carnations, tuberoses, and tulips, but says that wildflowers are best because of their natural origin. The book goes on to say that white roses attract health, counter bad vibes, and permit all that is positive; red roses are related to love, passion, desire, and spiritual stability. *Santa Muerte: Novena e historia de su culto* (n.d.), however, says that one can use whatever flowers one chooses, provided that they are removed when they become dry. The flowers capture the negative energy that surrounds one; in Mexico, this is said of the aloe vera plant. Red flowers are related to amorous wellbeing and happiness with one's partner. White flowers are related to health, wellbeing, and purification. Yellow flowers are related to economic achievements and money.

A cigarette, or tobacco in general, the more natural the better, should be used to purify one's Santa Muerte statue. Tobacco has its origin in pre-Hispanic America, and its use in traditional medicine and spirituality is well known. The cigar (*puro*) or cigarette (*cigarro*) should be lit and the smoke blown over the statue (*Santa Muerte: Novena e historia de su culto*, n.d.). *Culto a la Santa Muerte* (n.d.) describes cigarettes as of great importance to the altar to Santa Muerte; one is for the devotee, and one for La Santísima Muerte. The cigarette removes the envy that surrounds one at work or in the family. It is also suggested to smoke a cigar with Santa Muerte; this helps to purify the altar, and to remove all the negative energy in the environment.

Alcohol is offered with much love, for giving thanks, and in occasions when a boon has been granted. It should be changed once or twice a week. Preferred types of alcohol are tequila, rum, *aguaardiente* (hard water/PGA), brandy, and mezcal (*Culto a la Santa Muerte*, n.d.; *Santa Muerte: Novena e historia de su culto*, n.d.).

Ritual and Prayer

Included in the Santa Muerte books written and published by devotees, mostly anonymously, as these books tend to be compilations rather than the authors' own work, are a number of prayers, rituals, and spells. There are instructions for constructing an altar to Santa Muerte, and for spiritually cleansing or consecrating the altar before use (Galindo García & Galindo Flores, 2006).

There are the prayers and devotions that follow the Catholic tradition, including the novena (the nine-day prayer), the ejaculatory, the "Our Father" or Lord's Prayer, the Gloria, the rosary, the contemplated mysteries (joyful, painful, glorious, and luminous), as well as the Ten Commandments of Santa Muerte (González Olivo, 2009). If the offerings given to Santa Muerte are presented in a fairly informal manner, like a gift to a friend, some of the prayers are often highly structured in the form of petitions. Below are some of the prayers and rituals, though space limitations mean that they cannot be examined in depth:

Prayers:
prayer of invocation
to resolve conflict
to ask advice
to solve family problems
to stop economic problems
for abundance and finance
for bodily health
to stop a vice
to protect one's children
to avoid robberies
to protect one's job
for business
to protect one's business
to clean one's business
for luck
to attract good fortune in one's business and home

to attract a love

For protection during travel (González Olivo, 2009).

Spells:

The hand of Santa Muerte

the ritual of protection: the five-pointed star and salt

the ritual of the Three Deaths for protection

to get rid of the negative energy that surrounds us

ritual to receive money with the help of Santa Muerte

recipe to attract money

attract money with the advice of Santa Muerte

ritual to pay a debt

ritual to get your partner's help in paying a debt

ritual to better one's economic position

ritual to free one's self from debt

to resolve arguments or disagreements

so that negativity does not enter one's home or business

to win a pending trial

for health

to heal all sickness

to prevent "provoked" sickness from entering one's home

for the health of a loved one

for love

ritual for love with flowers

to have luck in love

To attract love (González Olivo, 2009).

It can be seen from these prayers, rituals, and spells that many of the requests made by devotees are of a material and worldly nature (Thompson, 1998). While this aspect does not much speak to the transcendent nature of spiritual practice, it says much about the socioeconomic status of many of the devotees. I've noticed that many

Mexicans do not pray for money, but for work. As well, asking God for things of this world is quite Catholic. "Many folk saints inhabit marginalized communities, the needs of which are more worldly than others; they therefore frequently act in a more worldly, more pragmatic, less dogmatic fashion than their official counterparts" (Griffith, 2003).

[M]any folk devotions begin through the clouding of the distinction between praying *for* and praying *to* a recently deceased person. If several family members and friends pray at someone's tomb, perhaps lighting candles and leaving offerings, their actions arouse the curiosity of others. Some give it a try—the *for* and the *to* begin intermingling because the frequent visits to the tomb suggest that the soul of its occupant may be miraculous. As soon as miracles are announced, often by family members and friends, newcomers arrive to send up prayers, now *to* the miraculous soul, with the hope of having their requests granted (Graziano, 2006).

The Church and the Shrine

In the past, devotion to Santa Muerte was practiced privately mostly, even secretly, at shrines and altars in the home. This all changed on *Día de los Muertos* (Day of the Dead, November first) in 2001 when Sra. Enriqueta Romero, better known as Doña Queta, placed a life-size statue of Santa Muerte in a glass box shrine in front of her building in the notoriously dangerous Barrio Tepito (Velázquez, 2009; Chestnut, 2012). There are a number of public shrines throughout Mexico and especially in Mexico City, but none are as significant, both in terms of traffic and importance, as Doña Queta's shrine in Calle Alfarería of Barrio Tepito (Rellea, 2008; Garma, 2009; Velázquez, 2009).

On the first of each month, and with more energy and greater numbers on the first of November, thousands of devotees gather in

41

the streets of Barrio Tepito to recite the Rosary to Santa Muerte, to have their statues blessed, and to pay respect to "the Saint of Tepito" (Chestnut, 2012). Doña Queta, with microphone in hand, acts as emcee, and is responsible for guiding the Rosary and prayers to Santa Muerte for over an hour: "Holy Death: I believe in you because you are just; as you take a young man or an old man, rich or poor" (Villarreal, 2009). The devotees hold hands and bow their heads; the act is truly communitarian, transpersonal. The atmosphere is cordial, respectful, and familiar; there are the occasional pot smokers, sharing joints with their friends, and the *activos* inhaling solvents from rags drenched with paint thinner, etc., but I have never seen any trouble (Villarreal, 2009).

Santa Muerte statues held aloft by devotees,
Barrio Tepito, Mexico City, November 1, 2011.

Doña Queta says that she is not a priestess, but a simple devotee like the others. She claims to have been practicing devotion to Santa Muerte since being introduced to Her by her aunt in 1962. The aged grandmother and "godmother" of the cult is low-key and affable (Velázquez, 2009; Chestnut, 2012), if a bit rough around the edges.

Devotion to Santa Muerte has little, if any, official organization. Devotion is typically practiced informally at either private or public shrines. However, one personality bears mention simply because of the volume and frequency of his presence in the media. Ex-Catholic Monsignor David Romo is the Archbishop and Primate of *La Iglesia Católica Apostólica Tradicional Mex-USA* (The Traditional Catholic Apostolic Church Mexico-USA). Romo is a married father of five and a veteran of the Mexican Air Force, in which he served as a clerk. He is also the self-professed leader and spokesman of the Santa Muerte cult. Since 2002, he has been leading masses at the National Sanctuary of Santa Muerte, located at Calle de

Bravo 35 in Colonia Morelos of Mexico City which is part of Barrio Tepito. Romo has claimed an attendance of 200-300 parishioners, mostly young people, at each mass. The masses are held at midnight (Chestnut, 2012).

Romo, the flamboyant and outspoken, high priest of Santa Muerte is also a tireless defender of the cult. When Sr. Martín Rábago, head of the *Conferencia del Episcopado Mexicano* (Mexican Episcopal Conference-CEM), and Cardinal Rivera Carrera called the practice of devotion to Santa Muerte "Satanic," Romo filed a defamation complaint with the *Ministerio Público* (Public Ministry). Martín Rábago stated that he would request the *Secretaría de Gobernación* (Secretary of the Interior-SEGOB) to review the process of religious registration. Romo then replied that the practice of devotion to Santa Muerte is no different from devotion to saints in other churches. Romo argued that Santa Muerte is a tool for evangelizing people in the marginalized sectors of society just as the Virgin of Guadalupe was a vehicle for converting indigenous Mexicans. At the time, SEGOB refused to intervene (Villarreal, 2009).

However, in April of 2005, despite protest marches by Santa Muerte devotees the previous month to the Zócalo, Mexico City's main square, and to Los Pinos, the presidential residence, SEGOB concluded in a 25-page resolution that *La Iglesia Católica Apostólica Tradicional Mex-USA* did not meet the qualifications for a religion and removed it from the list of recognized religions. Romo issued a call for Santa Muerte devotees to vote against the *Partido Acción Nacional* (National Action Party-PAN) in the 2006 Mexican Presidential Elections. Romo also held a series of meetings with Mexico City politicians to promote social development and community service projects that would be undertaken by Santa Muerte devotees of his church under the new organization, *Asociación Nacional de Altares y Santuarios de la Santa Muerte* (National Association of Altars and Sanctuaries of Santa Muerte), replacing *La Iglesia Católica Apostólica*

Tradicional Mex-USA. The organization was said to include 100 of the 120 altars that display Santa Muerte statues in Mexico City (Villarreal, 2009).

The legal action generated a large amount of press attention, which placed Romo in the spotlight. The priest even officiated the wedding of Mexican-Cuban television star Niurka Marcos (Chestnut, 2012). However, outside of Romo's own congregation, it is difficult to say how many devotees actually consider him a leader.

In something of an about-face, in 2007, Romo changed the name and image of Santa Muerte in his church to that of the Angel of Death, depicted as a white woman with brunette hair and wings to a seeming lukewarm response by the devotees (Chestnut, 2012).

An article printed in *Milenio* newspaper (Jiménez, 2009) says that a temple to Santa Muerte is being built in Mexico City. The temple is to include 500 seats, crypts, and a baptistery. The cost of the temple is said to be $38 million pesos, and construction is to be completed by 2010. David Romo, speaking on behalf of *La Iglesia Católica Apostólica Tradicional Mex-USA*, says that the temple will be the first world temple to Santa Muerte. The altar will contain three images, that of Christ, that of Santa Muerte, and that of an angel. The temple is also to have a recording and television studio to make broadcasts for the faithful via the internet. David Romo said that the building "will mark a watershed between past discrimination towards our faith by some intolerant and reactionary sectors, and will end the era of disintegration of the devotees of Santa Muerte" (Jiménez, 2009). At the time of the writing of this book, no such construction has begun.

In an even bigger development, it was reported in early 2011 that between December 18 and 20 of 2010 David Romo was arrested and charged with being a member of a gang of kidnappers by the Attorney General of the Federal District of Mexico (Pérez Arellano, 2011).

Is this testament to the inherent evil of the Santa Muerte cult, or a self-fulfilling media prophecy? Taking into account the notoriously endemic nature of corruption in Mexican law and politics, it is difficult to ascertain the veracity of these charges. But probably the charges will not harm the reputation of Santa Muerte or her devotees any more than has already been done.

The Catholic Church Versus Santa Muerte

Santa Muerte or *Muerte Santa*? A fine but important distinction exits in Spanish Catholicism between the concepts of *Santa Muerte* and *Muerte Santa*. A *Muerte Santa* is the hoped for 'good death' or 'holy death' of a Catholic who has confessed and received the Last Rites before dying. From here the lines blur. Santa Muerte as a personification of death, some say, is a confusion of the former term.

The Catholic Church understands believers of different alternatives of worship, but as to Santa Muerte, warns that "death is not a character, and does not save, or bring anything good, but instead is an act of idolatry practiced to a skeleton with a scythe, which is rejected by God since the Old Testament. The Church says that this is devil worship," says Father Del Rio (García Meza, 2008).

As for the myth that Santa Muerte grants favors or performs miracles, the priest said that "the devil is a good healer, and divines many things, not for free but, for the price of the precious souls of those who receive the service of the devil through his intermediaries. For practicing idolatrous worship they receive death by idol worship. Those who practice the cult of Santa Muerte are bound with diabolical ties. They are in debt and committed to the devil, and the devil is going to charge. The devil does not provide free services," says Father Del Rio (García Meza, 2008).

Such strong opposition by the Catholic Church to the cult of Santa Muerte is understandable considering the waning numbers of parishioners attending mass in Mexico today. Many of my own patients in Barrio Tepito, the Santa Muerte devotional epicenter, feel that the Church no longer addresses their needs.

José Luis Del Rio, pastor of the Chapel of Ojo de Agua in Saltillo, Coahuila says that "people confuse having a holy death (*Muerte Santa*) with the Holy Death (*Santa Muerte*). The holy death is when a person dies spiritually well prepared, because he or she has received the last spiritual sacraments, sacramental confession, the Eucharist by the *viaticum* [provision for a journey], the anointing of the sick, and so has a holy death. Now they reverse the adjective and make holy death like a character" (García Meza, 2008). The priest goes on to say that Santa Muerte is not recognized by the Church and that those who venerate her are ignorant, superstitious sinners.

For the Methodist Church in Mexico, which is quite small, Santa Muerte "is a devotion that has been emphasized greatly in recent years, is a popular belief, and we respect that belief, but do not see this being as something with authority of any kind, but is a fervor some people have because they want to believe in something. We do not believe in that, but we respect it," says Pastor Noé Gámez, head of the Temple Mesías, of the Methodist Church (García Meza, 2008).

In the article, "El culto a la Santísima Muerte, un boom en México" [The cult of Santa Muerte, a boom in Mexico] (n.d.), in the popular markets (*mercados municipals*) of Mexico, where you can buy herbs, candles, and religious items to combat the evil eye and all kinds of witchcraft, one can find Santa Muerte, next to the traditional images of the saints of Catholicism. You can find spells and prayers to ask for favors, melding pagan religious syncretism with Catholicism. All this caused the Catholic Church of Mexico to condemn the cult of Santa Muerte. In their official publication *Desde la Fe* (*From the Faith*) the Church refused to be part of the Santa Muerte religion and warned its parishioners against the cult.

The Catholic Church sees the cult of Santa Muerte as a heresy of popular Catholicism that is not accepted by the Roman Catholic Church. The warnings of the clergy against the practice say that death is not a person but a stage of life (Garma, 2009). "It's not un-Catholic to pray for a holy death. So, in the mind of some Mexicans, Santa Muerte might be seen as very Catholic" (Matovina, 2002). And so it is that most of the Mexican devotees to Santa Muerte see themselves as good Catholics. In all of this talk, there seems to be a notion that devotees of Santa Muerte are ignorant or misguided. While many devotees are from the less-educated social strata, there is little reason to believe that they are stupid or incapable of making decisions for themselves. There are well-educated and middle and upper-class devotees as well.

The Socioeconomic Context for the Practice of Devotion to Santa Muerte

Considering the low socioeconomic status of many of Santa Muerte's devotees, who are often the poor, taxi drivers, police, prostitutes, homosexuals, and others who live on the margins of society, devotion to Santa Muerte is often seen as a way to provide that which other saints have not or will not provide (Villarreal, 2009).

There are a few articles that deal with the boom in sales of Santa Muerte paraphernalia. An article printed on All Saints Day (also Day of the Dead and Santa Muerte's feast day) in 2008 in the newspaper *El Siglo de Torreon* in the Mexican state of Coahuila talks of this day also being the feast day of Santa Muerte. Though this is not recognized by the Church, many venerate her on this day. The article refers to Santa Muerte as "La Niña Blanca" (The White Girl) (García Meza, 2008). The article goes on to describe the various Santa Muerte paraphernalia available for sale in Saltillo's Mercado Juárez, including perfumes to invoke and request help from her. Sales of these products, including statues of the saint costing between $10 and $1500 pesos, are booming. All Saints Day, or Santa Muerte's feast day, is no different from any other day when these objects sell well. These products are purchased by people of all ages, sexes, and social classes.

Isidro Sánchez, a *comerciante* who sells religious objects in the mercado, says that the candle of seven powers is a best-seller. This candle is comprised of seven layered colors, white, red, black, yellow, blue, green, and purple, and each color pertains to different powers. Curiously, market vendor Susana Paulina Hernández, reported that her biggest Santa Muerte sales day was June 6, 2006; that is 06.06.06 (García Meza, 2008), but this seems on par with other sensational media representations that I will address later.

A female devotee named anonymously as "Gris" [Gray], says that she first encountered Santa Muerte in the state of Zacatecas. She claims that Santa Muerte addresses her needs more effectively than other saints. She must first ask permission of God before invoking Santa Muerte, but said that She provides her with protection, health, love, and whatever she wants (García Meza, 2008).

An article in *El Porvenir* newspaper (Harden Cooper, 2008) reports on the good sales of Santa Muerte paraphernalia in Mercado Juárez of Monterrey. These articles include candles that cost $20 pesos, to incense, prayers, and artisanal figures of Santa Muerte ranging from three centimeters to three feet tall in common cases, and even life-size figures at a height of 165 centimeters costing upwards of $7000 pesos.

Jackeline Rodriguez, known as Santus Sacerdotus Mortus, (Santa Muerte Priestess) a vendor in the market says, "She has many attributes and most times she can be assimilated as a religious image, but many people will not accept her. She is a being that helps you realize your request; people usually ask for love, money, work, as needed," (Harden Cooper, 2008). As mentioned previously, the needs of some devotees are more worldly and practical than those of others.

An article written in *El Universal* (2009 April, 10) by Carlos Garma, a research anthropologist at UNAM, refers to the cult of Santa Muerte as what anthropologists call a "cult of crisis." It has spread during a social and economic crisis that has hit hard the lives of many people in the most disadvantaged sectors of Mexican society (Garma, 2009). Religions have always thrived in these situations because they offer a spiritual outlet for the problems that people face daily. The cult of Santa Muerte attracts like a magnet people who face situations without a resolution, or those who are greatly disadvantaged socially.

The image of the Santa Muerte cult is viewed negatively by many Mexicans. People of higher economic strata view the cult with disdain, as a superstition of ignorant poor people, with the exception of some artists and politicians who have come to the rites, often clandestinely. The other churches (Catholic and Protestant) see this as a religious practice of witchcraft, an evil which must be condemned as a hoax (Garma, 2009).

An area that begs comparison and further investigation is the similarity of Santa Muerte and the Hindu Tantric deity or *devi* Kali. In the last age (Kali Yuga), when the end seems near and death and destruction are all around us, is it so strange to embrace death? Death is coming to us all, whether we like it or not.

Santa Muerte in the Media

The overwhelming majority of what has been written about Santa Muerte, in both Mexico and the United States, relates to her following among the criminal classes. News reports involving Santa Muerte are, as a rule, sensationalistic. They range from intolerant to idiotic. Parallels can be drawn between the media's coverage of Santa Muerte and of Islam as of late, where the actions of some devotees of either religion are made to speak ill of the whole community.

An article that a colleague sent to me during this study is a good example of Santa Muerte's media image. The article, printed in *The Guardian* (Larios, 2012), alleges that a poor family in Nacozari, Sonora, Mexico sacrificed three victims to Santa Muerte. The men are described as "trash pickers," and the women, "suspected of prostitution" (Larios, 2012). The family is suspected of being part of a cult that sacrificed two ten-year-old boys and a 55 year old woman to Santa Muerte. This article, like many others, says that Santa Muerte is "a figure adored mostly by outlaws," and that Santa Muerte is condemned by the Roman Catholic Church (Larios, 2012). It is thought that this is the first occurrence of ritual human sacrifice to Santa Muerte. The throats and wrists of the victims were cut with knives and axes, their blood spread on a Santa Muerte altar, and their bodies were buried near and beneath the dirt floors of the shacks of the alleged cult members. However, at the time of the article's publication, those arrested had not been charged with any crime. Jose Larrinaga, a spokesman for the State of Sonora Attorney General's Office, said that the family is part of a "cult," that they thought that offering blood to Santa Muerte would protect them and bring them money, and that they identify themselves as "fanatic followers of Santa Muerte" (Larios, 2012).

Another article claims that the cult of Santa Muerte is nothing new, that it is not connected to Catholicism or to Santería, as is sometimes thought. The cult of Santa Muerte is connected to ancient Mexican beliefs, especially of the Méxicas who, as part of their beliefs, maintain the cult of the old gods including Mictlantecuhtli and Mictecacíhuatl, the "lord and lady of darkness and death, who were entrusted with the dead" (García Meza, 2008).

The article goes on to talk about El Comandante Pantera (Commandant Panther) or Padrino Endoque (Godfather Endoque), leader of a Santa Muerte temple in Tultitlán, State of Mexico who was mysteriously gunned down with several high powered machine guns while sitting in his SUV (García Meza, 2008).

In the article "El culto a la Santísima Muerte, un boom en México" [The cult of Santa Muerte, a boom in Mexico] (n.d.), "drug traffickers have always been very religious; these individuals are not atheists. They are very superstitious," said Jose Maria Infante, doctor of psychology and director of research at the Faculty of Philosophy at the University of Nuevo León (García Meza, 2008). Infante added that *narcos* have always had their own cults and they find in Santa Muerte an image that represents them. "It is a figure that is very consistent with their activities where life and death are closely linked," said Infante (García Meza, 2008). He says that drug dealers are aware that in such activity they can die at any time, that for them life and death are everyday experiences, because they know that sometimes they have to kill or to be killed. To many, association with Santa Muerte has become evidence that a person is linked to organized crime, said the psychologist. So that's what the TSA dude thought of me when I passed through US Customs in San Jose, California. I was wearing a jacket and tie. I was attending a psychological conference, yet he labeled me, "One of those Santa Muerte people," because of an image in my luggage. He noted that drug traffickers seek in Santa Muerte magic solutions to their problems (García Meza, 2008).

Father Garza is a priest of the Church of Guadalupe in the border town of Anáhuac, Nuevo León, where in mid-2004, on the border highway from Anáhuac to Nuevo Laredo, Tamaulipas, a small shrine dedicated to the Virgin of Guadalupe was burned and partially destroyed. While on the Anáhuac-Lampazos highway, a route often used by drug traffickers, was built a shrine where a figure of Santa Muerte stands almost a meter high. "The flowering of drug trafficking on the border with the United States is causing an increase in the cult of Santa Muerte," says the priest (El culto a la Santísima Muerte, un boom en México, n.d.).

Francisco Javier Cantú Romero, spokesman for the Attorney General's Office (Procuraduría General de la República-PGR) in the state of Nuevo León, reported that in 2004 drug dealers were captured who had several altars to Santa Muerte. In late December the police arrested the leader of the gang involved in drug trafficking known as *Los Norteños* [The Northerners], who were identified by the police as a gang engaged in drug trafficking in the states of Jalisco, Morelos, and Veracruz. Among the firearms seized from the arrest was a gold .38 caliber pistol with precious stones and a figure of Santa Muerte (El culto a la Santísima Muerte, un boom en México, n.d.).

Much has been written about the criminal nature of the believers of Santa Muerte. Her popularity in prisons cannot be denied. However, it should be noted that, currently, the followers include members of very dissimilar families. People of all occupations and social classes can be seen at public Santa Muerte ceremonies and rituals (Garma, 2009).

The US media, while featuring fewer articles about Santa Muerte, is no less sensationalistic than her Mexican counterpart. A 2007 article (Ramirez, September 30) in the *Chicago Tribune* titled "'Saint Death' comes to Chicago: Some Mexicans put their faith in the skeletal icon Santa Muerte. But Catholic clergy say their belief in the icon should die," is quite telling of the existing prejudice.

Most famous among Santa Muerte's bad press is the arrest in 1998 of Daniel Arizmendi López, known as *el Mochaorejas* [the ear-chopper], who was a kidnapper that sent his victims' ears to family members in order to collect ransom. When López was arrested, the police allowed him to take his Santa Muerte statue with him to prison (García Meza, 2008; Chestnut, 2012).

Articles have been written about the popularity of devotion to Santa Muerte among prisoners (Castellanos, 2004), the poor (Johnson, 2004), taxi drivers, the police (Villarreal, 2009), prostitutes, drug dealers (Gonzáles Rodríguez, 2001; Cevallos, 2004), and various criminals (Gray, 2007; Chestnut, 20012), and of satanic sacrifices to protect drug traffickers (Dávila, 2003). There is, however, little mention in the media when a drug dealer or killer is arrested who has a shrine to the Virgin of Guadalupe in his home, as that is all too common.

The Archetype of Death

Every living thing will die eventually. Death is an inextricable counterpart to life. This inevitable fact of life is pushed aside by many, especially in the West. Fear of death lingers at the back of many minds. One's attitude toward death informs the ways in which one lives (Koestenbaum, 1971). Coming from Plato's *Ideas*, or primordial prototypes, Jungian archetypes are symbols in the collective unconscious that reside in each individual (Jung, 1972). As an archetype, the symbol of death is prolific throughout every culture.

Chapter 3: Research Methods

The purpose of this qualitative autoethnography is to explore the question: What is the individual's lived experience of the practice of devotion to Santa Muerte in the daily lives of her devotees in Mexico City? Some of the areas of research included are personal devotional practices and how they relate to the larger devotional community, a deeper look at the use of magic and ritual, connections between devotion and transcendence of the fear of death (or death itself), and the implications for the practice of psychotherapy in Mexico City. In this study, the practice of devotion to Santa Muerte is defined as engaging in devotional practices to Santa Muerte that include veneration, prayer, acts, and rituals. The research approach is qualitative and the research strategy is autoethnography.

Philosophical Assumptions of Research Design

The philosophical assumptions that guide this study are the constructivist and transpersonal paradigms which overlap and complement one another. Ontologically, constructivism assumes that the world is formed through people's meaning-making activities, and that these meanings are socially-constructed, subjective, varied, and multiple (Creswell, 2003; Mertens, 2005). Epistemologically, constructivism sees the research process as an interactive exchange between the researcher and the participants in the study (Mertens, 2005). The methodology of constructivism is qualitative, using researcher observation and open-ended interviews to generate thick and rich narratives of the lived experience of both researcher and participants. In this methodology, the lives and contexts of the researcher and participants are seen as important components of the study. Constructivist methodological strategies employed are the use of open-ended interviews, observation, and reflection. While constructionism is interested in cultural artifacts produced within a group, constructivism is more interested in the learning that an individual experiences within a group.

This study is also guided by the philosophical assumptions of the transpersonal paradigm (i.e., working through and going beyond the personal/egoic state to encompass a more whole, unitive state). Ontologically, the transpersonal paradigm holds that there is a transcendent dimension beyond the limited self and beyond the mundane that, when accessed, can enrich more conventional research methods. Epistemologically, the knower and the known and objective and subjective positions are tenuous and interrelated. Transpersonal methodology includes the use of intuition and direct knowing. That transformation of the researcher and research participants may occur through the research process is also considered (Anderson & Braud, 1998).

Research Design

I conducted this study using the qualitative research design of autoethnography. Autoethnography comes out of the traditions of autobiography and ethnography. "Autoethnography is a form of self-reflection and writing that explores the researcher's personal experience and connects this autobiographical story to wider cultural, political, and social meanings and understandings" (Ellis, 2004). "Autoethnography is an approach to research and writing that seeks to describe and systematically analyze (graphy) personal experience (auto) in order to understand cultural experience (ethno)" (Ellis, Adams, & Bochner, 2010).

This design is a method for understanding and honoring shared cultural experience through individual lived experience through a lens that is interested, subjective, and personal. The method is story rather than theory driven (Ellis, Adams, & Bochner, 2010). Through autoethnography and transpersonal theory, I am looking for particular subjective experiences rather than universal objective "laws." As an autoethnographer, I am interested in the thick, rich descriptions that participants tell of their experience, allowing the influences of subjectivity, emotion, and my own connection to the phenomenon.

At the same time, I want to tell my own story relating to the phenomenon of practicing devotion to Santa Muerte. In telling my story, I do so critically and analytically. This involved collecting and analyzing, comparing and contrasting, the stories of other members of the cult.

My undergraduate degree from Harvard University is in Literature and Creative Writing. In writing this qualitative autoethnographic study, I utilize story-telling devices such as narrative, plot, and characters (Ellis, Adams, & Bochner, 2010). Personal epiphanies also play a role in the writing of this study. Narrative tools, such as "showing" (Ellis, Adams, & Bochner, 2010) and dialog, help to bring readers into scenes in evocative and emotional ways.

Most often through the use of conversation, showing allows writers to make events engaging and emotionally rich. "Telling" is a writing strategy that works with "showing" in that it provides readers some distance from the events described so that they might think about the events in a more abstract way. Adding some "telling" to a story that "shows" is an efficient way to convey information needed to appreciate what is going on, and a way to communicate information that does not necessitate the immediacy of dialogue and sensuous engagement (Ellis, Adams, & Bochner, 2010).

In this way, I weave together my story with those of participants to create a rich and varied text. I use vignettes and scenes, as well as conversations that develop the "characters" of the participants.

As a psychotherapist, I typically give my patients writing or journaling assignments influenced by the Narrative Therapy work of

Michael White. I practice these exercises myself, as I believe that writing is therapeutic, is a way of coming to know what we are thinking, feeling, and what we want or do not want in our lives. When we create, write, or tell rich and thick stories about ourselves and our experience, we engage in "meaning-making," and we gain control of the narrative of our lives (White & Epston, 1990). It is through such narrative autoethnography that transformation of the researcher and the participants take place.

Indeed, psychotherapist Inga-Brit Krause (2003) of London's Tavistock Clinic believes that psychotherapists and ethnographers have much to learn from one another about how to ask questions. As psychotherapists, we often forget about our interrelatedness and the intersubjective space that we share with our patients. Too often is it that we fall into typical ruts with the types of questions that we ask. In short, we tend to find what we are looking for. We need to be open to the experience of the unexpected. As a writer, psychotherapist, devotee of Santa Muerte, and autoethnographer, I felt myself uniquely positioned to undertake this study.

Traditional ethnography has been criticized for being too distant from the cultures that it purports to study (Krause, 2003). Being an outsider to a culture that one is studying is necessarily problematic. Autoethnography addresses this gap, as I, the autoethnographer, am a part of the culture that that I am studying, I am also studying myself.

Ellis, Adams, & Bochner (2010) summarize autoethnography thusly: When researchers write autoethnographies, they seek to produce aesthetic and evocative thick descriptions of personal and interpersonal experience. They accomplish this by first discerning patterns of cultural experience evidenced by field notes, interviews, and/or artifacts, and then describing these patterns using facets of storytelling (e.g., character and plot development), showing and telling, and alterations of authorial voice. Thus, the autoethnographer not only tries to make personal experience meaningful and cultural experience engaging, but also, by producing accessible texts, she or he may be able to reach wider and more diverse mass audiences that traditional research usually disregards, a move that can make personal and social change possible for more people (Ellis, Adams, & Bochner, 2010).

It is this broadening of the readership that especially appeals to me. Who reads academic texts? Other academics. Period.

Criticism of the Autoethnographic Method

While some researchers advocate autoethnography for its value, others contend that there are also several concerns about the method. Chang (2008) warns autoethnographers of pitfalls that they should avoid in doing autoethnography: "(1) excessive focus on self in isolation from others; (2) overemphasis on narration rather than analysis and cultural interpretation; (3) exclusive reliance on personal memory and recalling as a data source; (4) negligence of ethical standards regarding others in self-narratives; and (5) inappropriate application of the label autoethnography" (p. 54).

I have avoided becoming an academic for such reasons as this person above describes. What a waste of time, just to have a "say," to make a "name" for oneself. It's ludicrous, the whole "publish or perish" mentality of academia. And I refuse to participate in it. My job is psychotherapy. I work to help people. I do not give a shit about the above person's academic concerns or career ambitions. I learned very early in school that to write a really successful essay that would get you a good grade, was to attack, to find some lack, something wrong, and then take it apart like a mechanic. That's how you become a really good academic.

Some qualitative researchers have expressed their concerns about the worth and validity of autoethnography. Robert Krizek

(2003) contributed a chapter, "Ethnography as the Excavation of Personal Narrative" to the book *Expressions of Ethnography*, in which he expresses concern about the possibility for autoethnography to devolve into narcissism.

Really, if you are not a narcissist, you are a failure as a human being. Lots of people have their pet theories (and can never seem to grow and gain new ones). OK, falling in love with your own reflection to the point of obsession is not a good thing. But, for God's sake, fall in love with your own reflection! Love yourself! Be amazed by yourself! Krizek goes on to suggest that autoethnography, no matter how personal, should always connect to some larger element of life" (Krizek, 2003). Maybe this dude got tenure after writing this. I sure hope so! Because we certainly need more professors. Of course, I am being sarcastic.

This author/researcher does not want to fall into narcissism, and while I have not personally noticed these above aspects in other autoethnographic studies, I noted how they can present obstacles to be overcome and was mindful of them during my research.

Rationale for Selecting Design

The reason for selecting this design was due to my personal circumstances, that I am a devotee of Santa Muerte, and an interested participant-observer of the phenomenon that I wanted to study. The story of how I came to the practice of devotion to Santa Muerte is a rather long one that I wished tell in depth. For now, I will limit myself to a few comments.

As a volunteer, I practice psychotherapy at a low-cost community mental health clinic in Barrio Tepito of Mexico City where the first public and most important shrine to Santa Muerte is located. In this study, I want to tell my own story of the practice of devotion to Santa Muerte and how it may or may not fit with the stories of other devotees. There is an undeniable cultural element to this phenomenon, but I wanted to go beyond ethnography to study my connection to these cultural practices.

Validity Parameters

In autoethnographic studies, reliability rests on the narrator's credibility. "For autoethnographers, validity means that a work seeks verisimilitude; it evokes in readers a feeling that the experience described is lifelike, believable, and possible, a feeling that what has been represented could be true" (Ellis, Adams, & Bochner, 2010). The validity and trustworthiness of this study's findings will be assured by intuition, prolonged engagement (i.e., the researcher is deeply involved with the subject of inquiry for an extended period of time), persistent observation, and thick description. Credibility, transferability (i.e., that research findings are applicable across contexts), dependability, and confirmability (i.e., results are supported by research participants) will be assured by member-checking and triangulation of themes (i.e., cross-verification) generated by thematic analysis of the participants' narratives (Creswell, 2003; Mertens, 2005; Williams, 2011).

Sampling and Participant Selection

The twelve participants for this study were recruited through a process of purposeful sampling (Creswell, 2003) to select those participants best able to help me understand the individual's experience of the practice of devotion to Santa Muerte in the daily lives of her devotees in Mexico City. The participants were recruited through flyers posted or distributed in certain areas where devotees were likely to see them (e.g., near the shrine to Santa Muerte in Barrio Tepito of Mexico City and in Barrio Tepito generally). I also asked for volunteers by word-of-mouth, as the spoken word carries more weight in Mexico than does the printed word. The participants were all 18 years or older, of sound mind and body.

Procedure

After willing participants were located and selected through purposeful sampling, the participants were presented with an informed consent form to read and sign. An initial, open-ended interview (approximately one hour) was conducted and recorded with the possibility of a follow-up interview. Interviews were transcribed from tape recordings, and presented to participants for verification. The transcribed recordings were then translated from Spanish to English. The content of the interviews were analyzed thematically.

I also used observational field notes collected in a researcher journal, as well as insights gained through dreams and meditation which were noted in a personal diary.

Ethical Considerations

The whole study is designed considering the ethical protection of participants along APA guidelines, to minimize risks and enhance benefits to participants and all involved with the study. I employed an informed consent form, and maintained confidentiality and protection of data. Efforts were made to avoid minimal risk to participants.

As to "relational ethics" (Ellis, Adams, & Bochner, 2010), that I live near and am in ways connected to the community that I studied, I believe that, as a researcher in Mexico writing for an English-speaking audience in the United States, I am far enough removed so as to not cause harm to participants.

Possible benefits to all involved with the study include the therapeutic effects that accrue to participants being given a voice and being listened to and heard, clarifying beliefs of participants, and personal and transpersonal transformation.

A possible criticism that could arise from this study is that I am a white, American male, a *gringo* who is likely more educated and affluent than the majority of the participants in the study who were all Mexican and mostly of lower socio-economic status. In answering the criticism of possible exploitation from an outsider: I have been with my partner, who is Mexican, since 2007, and I plan to live in Mexico for the remainder of my days. I have lived in Mexico City since 2008. I have worked since 2009 as a volunteer psychotherapist at a low-cost community mental health clinic in Barrio Tepito, the epicenter of the phenomenon and an area so dangerous that most citizens of Mexico City would never go there. I speak Spanish fluently, and I am recognized in the community. While the practice of devotion to Santa Muerte is not organized in any official way, I attend November 1st feast days and I visit the main shrine in Calle Alfarería where I am known by its proprietor Doña Queta. I am a devotee of Santa Muerte. While I am not Mexican, I am a member of the devotional community of Santa Muerte, if there be such a community.

Data collection

I collected participant narratives through open-ended interviews. I used field notes and a researcher journal to note my own observations, thoughts, ideas, and reactions, as well as images, drawings, photos, poetry, creative expressions, insights gained from dreams, meditations, etc.

This has to be so boring for the reader to slog through. Again, you can just skip to the diary section. I understand completely. Editing this bores the hell out of me.

Treatment of Data

Data was treated by thematic analysis of participants' transcribed narratives gained from open-ended interviews. As far as biases and preconceptions, I am a devotee of Santa Muerte myself. I expected that there would be convergences and divergences between my ideas and those of participants.

Conclusion

In conclusion, the purpose of this qualitative autoethnography is to explore the question: What is the individual's experience of the practice of devotion to Santa Muerte in the daily lives of her devotees in Mexico City? Some of the areas of research included are personal devotional practices and how they relate to the larger devotional community, the use of magic and ritual, connections between devotion and transcendence of the fear of death (or death itself), and the implications for the practice of psychotherapy in Mexico City and beyond. The practice of devotion to Santa Muerte is defined as engaging in devotional practices to Santa Muerte that include veneration, prayer, acts, and rituals. The research approach is qualitative and the research strategy is autoethnography.

The data is presented in a narrative, novelistic form, relying largely on diary excerpts, where the stories of participants and my own are interwoven into an intersubjective tapestry. I am grateful to Dr. Mark McCaslin for the term postrepresentation, which helps to elucidate the path of this qualitative autoethnographic study.

Postrepresentation is "the process of transforming subjectively collected data into an intersubjective narrative. This transformation is brought about through the researcher's lens of experience being used as a filter for subjectively collected data taken from the participants of the research" (Dr. Mark McCaslin, personal communication, October 2013).

I, as the researcher, say "I" in the narrative telling of the story of the research. The participation of other devotees in this narrative may, indeed, be transformative for both parties and, beyond that, to the reader.

Chapter Four: The Diary of the of the Project

Monday, 26 March 2007:

Today she was my nurse. She took care of me lovingly and she hated and loved me alternately. I really believed that my head was going to explode from the altitude sickness. I want to take a picture so that I can remember or prove that it happened. The moment is so surreal. Alcohol kills germs and is the enemy and Montezuma's Revenge.

The crush of the crowds in the markets; Santa Muerte everywhere we look; music blasting from vendors and street musicians; the smells, overwhelming, change and morph into different smells every few feet we walk, carried forward through the stalls by the crowds. She squeezes my hand tighter. Her eyes dart back and forth. She begins to cry and hyperventilate. I pull her along to an alley that opens on an empty square; empty, because at the other end is Templo Mayor, the ancient Aztec temple and the navel of the world, and so there is no exit.

She was afraid. I told her that my friend Bill always asks, "What is the worst that can happen?" when faced with a fearful situation; then, he accepts that and he acts. She asked what the worst thing that could happen was. I paused, "Walking through the crowds." She smiled and squeezed my hand as we reentered the mass.

This girl was to later become my wife and partner.

Thursday, 29 March 2007:

I just got home from burying my best friend, Jacky, in Texas and loving my lover in Mexico. I don't know where to begin, where to start with the story. I suppose I can just give impressions.

I saw that she posted a picture of the two of us at the *Isla de las Muñecas*. She posted it as, "La belle et le bad boy on the island of dolls." I loved all of Mexico. I loved loving her. Walking around the base of the pyramid of the sun in the valley of the gods (Teotihuacan), kissing my Santa Muerte statue, all of this was golden. So very much! I could not experience it all. My love exceeds so many boundaries.

Friday, 30 March 2007:

The funeral was vulgar in many ways. Jacky's sister-in-law told some lame story about how it's all OK since Jacky was "saved" and so is not burning in hell. I leaned in to Bill, put my arm around his shoulder as he cried and said, "This is a bunch of crap." When the preacher said, "Death is not our friend, death is our enemy," I got up and went out for a smoke. Such garbage. Bill Boysen (as opposed to the previous Bill Senese) followed me out in short order. He, too, was disgusted. He said, "When will people evolve?" And, we smoked and talked.

Drinking away the night, talking and remembering with friends, my sister, crying and hugging one another. Bill and I talked about our speaking parts at the funeral, the power derived from me standing strong, invoking, and holding my hand on Jacky's coffin while he read his piece, of people approaching and saying, "Great eulogy. Thank you." All I could remember saying was, "Tell the people you love that you love them now. Don't wait."

The Mexicans that came to the funeral, the pretty Mexican girls crying over Jacky's death; he would have loved that. The presence of these lovely Mexican girls validated Jacky's stupid *cholo* moustache, the moustache that Jeff said looked like a bad magician.

Through these encounters and others, we caught glimpses of Jacky's other lives, mysterious and secret lives that he kept from us.

There were all these people who were devastated by his death and we never knew they existed.

Bill and I discussed various potential other lives, such as that Jacky was a secret agent and when he had asked where exactly was Iraq, it was a ruse, a cover, that he had actually worked in said country assassinating various Baathist politicians. We say these things jokingly, but there is a truth here—we're just not sure what it is.

The main point is that our friend was not completely honest with us; there was much that he kept from us. His family has his diaries that, unknown to me, he maintained since 1989. In these diaries, he is said to have meticulously chronicled his secret drug use, even going as far as budgeting his money to that end…coke, speed, heroin. We only knew about his sloppy beer drinking. I wonder what else we don't know.

Jacky, how little we knew you. Bill said that we were a part of Jacky's life, not the whole of it.

Sunday, 1 April 2007:

Today I was lying in bed and reading a book by Miguel Serrano about Hermann Hesse and Carl Jung when I heard a loud crash and the power went out. Immediately, a man began screaming, "Help me! Oh God, help me!" It sent shivers down my spine. I stood up and listened through the open window. The man seemed to be on the next street, maybe two hundred yards away. My heart was racing. I called 911 and explained what had happened. By the time I got off the phone, the screaming had stopped. I put on shoes and a jacket and went to see what had happened. I saw a group of men gathered around a lawn. I then saw a man sitting on the law. He had no shirt and his whole upper body was burned black. His head was black and his hair was burned away. Pink flesh hung from his arms. He sat shaking, looking inhuman. Police, fire, and ambulance arrived soon after. Apparently, the man touched a wire on a pole on the sidewalk. There was a large, black burned area on the pole.

Later tonight, I walked back over to the pole. I talked with a technician from the electric company. He told me that the man stuck a knife in the wire running down the pole. He didn't know why. He said that the man's shirt burned off and that pieces of shirt and skin where fused to the wire and the pole. He said that the man was lucky to be alive.

I said, considering the man's condition, that I wondered whether he wouldn't be better off dead. The technician turned to me and, very sincerely, said, "Don't ever say that. No one's better off dead."

Saturday, 21 July 2007:

My best friend died of a drug overdose in March. Every day brings a new and different sadness. People from the past contact me all the time, the late news of his death trickling down. He and I were very close. I guess that it why they seek me out and contact me. All of it is painful and complicated. I don't think I've taken enough time to process it all. It all comes at me like a train; it seems to move slowly, but it takes a very long time to stop, and the weight of it is crushing.

Tuesday, 28 April 2009:

There was a big earthquake yesterday. This was the most profound earthquake I had experienced. If you have not experienced an earthquake, the feeling is of extreme groundlessness. That is what is so scary: the very earth beneath you moves, so that there is no way to judge what is and is not. The high apartment building in which I live, in ground-zero Colonia Roma, frequently shakes and sways when large trucks path beneath. This was quite frightening initially, but it couldn't compare to yesterday. Still, I did nothing. I sat in the chair at my desk as the building swayed violently. Not being able to discern what is real is what is scary.

Sunday, 1 November 2009:

Santa Muerte: I am unsure what to say about all this. I haven't been able to write well or even to feel comfortable writing for a long time. I looked through the literature, and I definitely have PTSD (Post Traumatic Stress Disorder).

Last week I visited the Santa Muerte shrine in Colonia Morelos. I work in a mental health clinic in this colonia, the most dangerous in the city; this *colonia* is a part of the infamous Barrio Bravo de Tepito. My nine o'clock patient didn't show up, so I had time to kill until eleven.

It was overcast and gloomy, the first time that the sun wasn't sitting on top of this colonia. I had been wanting to visit this shrine for a long time. Generally, though, this area is a 'no go' zone for normal people. It is a haven for the poor, the criminal, the dispossessed. Normal Mexicans do not go to this colonia, much less do *güeros* (whites).

Devotion to Santa Muerte used to be a secret affair, with altars occupying a devotee's closet. The very old Sra. Romero changed all that by placing a shrine in the street. That was eight years ago. Now, each October 31 a thousand devotees flock to this shrine to pay homage to the statue of the saint (*La niña blanca* (the white girl), *Santisima Muerte* (Holiest Death), *La señora de la noche* (the lady of the night), etc.) all dressed in white like a dead bride.

Walking around this *colonia* in a suit and tie, a big red beard, and just generally being the only white person there, I got a lot of looks; one woman even yelled at me to get out. When I got lost and asked directions back to the clinic, people I stopped in the street seemed out of it, not even recognizing a street a few blocks away. Everything was wet, and I had to step over bodies of rotting dogs and homeless people wrapped in plastic.

When I finally found the shrine, I couldn't see the saint, as everything was being painted for the celebration on Saturday. I met the golden toothed Sra. Romero, the owner of the shrine, who was supervising the work. I told her that I was a devotee, and I asked if I could take photos. She was very hospitable and obliging. She hugged and kissed me, and gave me a calendar with a picture of the shrine, as she invited me to the celebration. After taking in the scene, I gave Sra. Romero a kiss on the cheek and went on my way.

Despite, and maybe because of, the stresses of life and obligations, I had to return to the shrine on Halloween. I figured I would get there at the five o'clock beginning, and be out of there before it got dark, long before the crescendo at midnight. I knew that it was usual for devotees to carry statues of the saint, even life-size ones; so, I carried a foot high Santa Muerte statue dressed in white (White is supposed to represent spiritual knowledge.) that was given me by a young male patient of mine.

When I arrived, the orations had just begun to call out over a loudspeaker hanging from a telephone pole. Around a thousand devotees were massed in the street, Calle de Alfareria, between Calles de Mineros and Panaderos.

The weather was dark and the mood was somber. Marijuana smoke was thick in the air, and I saw many smoking joints and drinking beer from caguamas (These are illegal acts, even in this city. But, Santa Muerte does enjoy a drink and marijuana is often used as incense.). There were no police around, because this is a lawless area since pre-Hispanic times (This is unusual in a city with machine gun carrying police on every block.).

I was nervous coming and going, but completely comfortable amongst the devoted. Everyone was more than nice; they handed out candy, chocolate skulls, incense, sprays to bless your statue, or your Santa Muerte tattoo. Young *chamacos* passed me big joints that I politely refused. Families with young children held hands in a circle as they recited the orations. We all held our statues aloft and chanted, "Santisima Muerte! Mujer de la noche!" People brought offerings of flowers, apples and apples covered in honey, tequila, marijuana, Cuban cigars, etc. People offered to pour tequila over my statue of the saint.

People generally misunderstand Santa Muerte. The Roman Church has waged war on her. Still, most devotees to the saint consider themselves Catholic. Supposedly, the origins of Santa Muerte date back to before the Spanish conquest of New Spain, correlating to Aztec gods, but the image is unmistakably of the European Grim Reaper. Even in typical fashion of the Roman Church's imperial conquest of adapting their new religion to the old ones they encountered, they left this gap open: Death.

Death is very important in Mexican society, as can be seen by the celebrations of *Dia de los Muertos*. Death is abundant in Mexico. Over 6,000 executions this year so far, and October has seen the highest body count of this grim year. While Santa Muerte is the saint of the prisoner, the drug dealer, the prostitute, the kidnapper and the kidnapped alike, the theme is fairly universal; death comes to us all, some of us will be more familiar with Her when we meet Her than will others. Long Live Death!

Tuesday, 3 November 2009:

I went to Ecatepec yesterday. Ecatepec is a municipality in the State of Mexico. The population of Ecatepec is around three million, the largest in the country. A colleague of mine recently told me that he saw a map of the early Spanish conquest, back when México City (Tenochtitlan) was an island in the middle of a lake. He said that one of the few place names on the mainland was Ecatepec, north of México.

I took the train there for the Santa Muerte celebration. It was in an area under a highway and metro train overpass. When I arrived, there was a *cumbia* band playing on a stage, the musicians in matching suits. Images of Santa Muerte were all around. Vendors were selling various Santa Muerte paraphernalia. I bought an elaborately hand drawn t-shirt with an image of Santa Muerte.

This is a dangerous area and I stick out. People stare at me and comment to each other. I feel nervous. I wonder if I made the right choice in coming all the way out here. The whole area is depressed, the buildings run down, and everything looks dirty, though the air seems cleaner. Young men covered with tattoos pass a joint and stare at me, nudging each other. Tattoos are not common in Mexico, except among the criminal class. I hike my shirt sleeves up to reveal my own tattoos, one of Santa Muerte, to hopefully but impossibly blend in in some way. When I feel most anxious, I see Doña Queta. She beams. We greet each other with a kiss. I feel like everyone sighs in relief, though it's probably just me. Anyway, any potential danger to me is now gone.

Poster ad for 2009 Santa Muerte celebration in Ecatepec.
Translation: Man by his very nature needs to nourish the spirit. The cult of Santa Muerte fortifies it. It respects any religious current, while demanding the same. We welcome the faithful who want to fortify the soul.

Thursday, 10 June 2010:

Santa Muerte comes up in the talk, as is often the case. I am the resident expert on the cult. I have come to a greater understanding of Her. She is the deity of change, of temporality in general, like Heraclitus saying that you can never step into the same river twice. The only constant is change; it's the only thing one can really be sure of. As I have observed in my own dreams and those of my patients, images of *La Muerte*, of death, most often presage change. Also in the Tarot card of death, the meaning is the same: change.

Wednesday, 10 November 2010:

Things are bad here in Mexico. I have been buying either *El Grafico* or *Metro* newspapers lately, and reading them on the train to the clinic. Sometimes I clip articles that I later share with an old friend during our Sunday talks. I think reading the newspapers may be a bad idea; the news is so bad every day.

There was an article today about a hundred families leaving their homes in Reynosa, Tamaulipas to escape the violence. And while the violence seems much worse in the northern states of Tamaulipas, Nuevo Leon, Coahuila, and Chihuahua, things are pretty bad here.

Two weeks ago, six or seven young men meeting late at night on a corner in Barrio Tepito to make the pilgrimage to the San Hipólito church for the benediction (held on every 28th) of San Judas Tadeo (the patron saint of desperate and lost causes) were gunned down with AK-47s (called in the papers *cuernos de chivas*, goat horns; likely because of their banana clips) and AR-15s (American military assault rifles). Then, over the weekend, a seventeen-year-old girl was gunned down with a *cuerno de chiva* two blocks from the clinic where I work. All of this is in the area where I work, and it concerns a lot of the patients that I see.

There's a kid of fifteen or sixteen years who passes by when I am outside the clinic smoking. He used to always be accompanied by more kids, and they would look at me and laugh, until they got more courage to talk to me. At that point, they would show me the joint they were passing, and offer me some. As always, I say that I have to work, and they respect this.

One of the kids tried to touch a cigarette lighter to my beard. I grabbed it out of his hand and threw it across the street. His friends all laughed, as he had to go looking for it.

After that, the kids have treated me with respect, especially the one aforementioned. He sometimes hangs around talking, asking me questions for long periods. He once told me that his father was in *Los Zetas* (one of the drug cartels), and was gunned down in Sinaloa, fifty odd shots, and some to the face. I don't know if this was true or if he was just trying to look cool.

This kid has always been cool with me, and he is like a lot of the patients I've seen. Even if he doesn't stop to talk, he will always shake my hand and ask how I am. Usually, he shows me his stash of weed.

Last week he offered me his makeshift apple pipe. As always, I say that I would like to smoke, but I have to work. "Yes, I understand, doctor," he says.

However, when I saw him today, he lifted his T-shirt to show me a black pistol tucked into his belt. The cigarette fell out of my mouth, and I must have looked pretty 'not calm' and 'not cool' for once. I asked if it was a nine. He said it was a 45. I was shaken, and, right after this my patients arrived and I had to take my leave, bumping fists with the kid as is the tradition there.

At least half of my session with this couple passed before I became aware that I wasn't listening. I thought that the Italian stiletto that I carry, that has saved me a few times, would mean nothing against a 45 automatic. I thought about how nice and respectful this kid is. I thought, "I need to have a talk with him." Then, "What would I say?" Then, I thought I want to give this kid a hug. And I nearly cried.

This was after a night on the phone convincing a teenage girl patient not to cut herself anymore until we could talk today.

Thursday, 16 June 2011:

I got up in the morning, and I wrote until two. Then, I went to Mercado San Juan to buy Santa Muerte candles, a white one for knowledge, and one black to counter enemies.

Friday, 11 January 2013:

Santa Muerte and Kali bear a striking resemblance to one another. Kali comes in the dark age of death and destruction, as does Santa Muerte. Kali is a manifestation of the *Devi*, the goddess, as Santa Muerte manifests as the Virgin's dark Other.

Tuesday, 6 August 2013:

The cat has been sick. He has had a lot of snot in his lungs. So, I suggested we take him to the vet. The antibiotics have been hard on him, not to mention the horror of having to force pills down his throat. He hasn't been eating. We have had to inject baby food into his throat with a syringe. This is not pleasant, but it's what is needed. I hold the cat while my wife feeds him. It works.

Today, she took me into the bedroom and closed the door to talk about putting him to sleep. I got so angry. She acts as though I don't care and that I have done nothing. She is the one with all the free time, and yet she shirks her responsibilities to the cat. Incredible! I am sure her mother or father put such a stupid idea in her head. I told her, like I continue to tell her, that the cat is going to get better and be with us for a long time still. We have to be positive! Being negative will harm the cat! Placebo vs. Nocebo! I know this to be true better than I know my own name.

I came out of the bedroom, and the cat was standing there. He probably heard all she said. Killing the cat? What the hell!? Before she came home, I swaddled the cat in a towel and fed him by myself. It was difficult, but I did it.

After this conversation, she went to teach at UNAM. I crushed up a sardine and presented it to the cat while chanting a mantra in my head. He ate that shit up! I nearly cried. Well, I did cry. The cat will live and thrive!

I can't stand this pessimism! Say *yes*, not *no*! I thanked Sri Ganesha, Sri Shiva, Mahadevi, and Santa Muerte for getting the cat to eat on his own. But maybe the cat heard my wife pronouncing his death sentence lest he eat, and he complied.

Her parents want to come with us to the vet tomorrow morning. I do not want that. They will create more chaos than there will be already. And I suspect that they are giving off negative vibes. I can't tolerate that. You say yes to life! You stay positive! You *know* that it will all work out for the best! I cannot tolerate a loser attitude! Mexicans are such pessimists!

When she came home tonight, the cat got up and began eating his sardine again. I immediately took her into the bedroom, closed the door, and said what I wrote above. She listened, because she saw the result she wanted. She needs to be on board in order to produce the desired result, not only acquiescing when it's already done.

I feel both sick and happy. I did not do this. I am just a conduit for the divine will. My part was surrendering to that will, being open to it. It is difficult to write about magic, but that's what this is.

Thursday, 29 August 2013:

Death is a mystery, perhaps the ultimate mystery. No one knows with any certainty what lies beyond the veil. Maybe this is why death has been portrayed in such dark terms. The Underworld is the typical description of the world of the dead. What is the Underworld like? It is dark, and thusly mysterious. It is said that the Aztec lord and lady of death live in a house with no windows. What could be more mysterious? She wears a cowl that covers Her form. Her form is skeletal, a form, a structure, the scaffolding that holds the meat suit that houses our soul. Her form is laid bare to relieve the mystery. We are all the same in form.

Thursday, 5 September 2013:

The earth is quaking all the time; I can feel it. It is unsettling, but I am unsure why.

Friday, 20 September 2013:

There were a bunch of drunk guys outside the Oxxo convenience store last night when I went to buy beer. They were looking at my tattoos, commenting, and showing me theirs. There was some trouble over my Santa Muerte tattoo. Some guy showed me his crucifix and said, "This is life!" He points at Santa Muerte and says, "That it death!" Fair enough. I'm glad that I stood tall and looked strong, that it didn't come to anything ugly.

Thursday, 26 September 2013:

Karma is the law of cause and effect. It is said that every cause carries within it its effects. Karma is the residue attaching to every action with which one identifies. If one abstains from action or does not identify with actions performed, no karma accrues. Karma is what keeps us bound to the wheel of Samsara (i.e., birth, life, death, re-birth, re-death). As long as there is karma (karmic debt), one will reincarnate (i.e., be made flesh again) on this plane of existence until all of these karmic debts are paid-in-full.

The law of *karma* is mysterious. It is very difficult to know what effects will manifest from a particular action. A good intention, giving birth to a particular action, can very easily manifest bad effects. It has been said that no one can take anything from you that you do not owe to them (e.g., perhaps you owe a debt to someone from a previous birth).

Anyway, clinging to what is "yours" increases misery; *I, me, mine*, are *kleshas*; see below. At the same time, you cannot give something to someone that you do not owe (e.g., We see this often when we try to do something nice for someone, or tell them something nice, and it does not work or falls on deaf ears. You owe nothing to these people; move on.).

The Five *Kleshas*, or obstructions, are egoism, ignorance, attachment, aversion, and clinging to life.

Egoism in the sense of *ahamkara* (i.e., *I*-identification, ego). Confusing the Self with the body-mind. There is no separation between subject and object.

Ignorance in the sense of not knowing/realizing that all is one.

Attachment to the fruits of one's actions; that one is the doer of actions.

Aversion: if all is God, what is impure, gross, or un-holy, etc.?

Clinging to life (Fear of Death) that is temporary is like trying to hold onto waves as they pass through your hands.

Saturday, 26 October 2013:

The internet is out again. I guess a branch fell and cut the fiber optic line. Then, the electric company came to replace a light pole and cut the fiber optic line again.

The repairmen from the internet company who came to the house to put in a new fiber optic line saw the Santa Muerte shrine in my office. One of them seemed scared by it, but it turned out that the other is a devotee from Ecatepec. He agreed to be interviewed for my research. He asked me if my Santa Muerte statue had a name. I didn't know what to say. "They have names?" "Depending on the particular figure," he said. I know that She has many names, as does Shiva, but I didn't know of a practice of naming *your* particular image of Her. By the time my research project was finally approved, I could not get in touch with the repairman. None of the other participant-devotees seemed to know anything of this naming of one's images. That doesn't mean that it's not a thing. So much of this is free-form, and I am not interested in what "everyone" does. I am more interested in personal devotion and practice, because that is where the truth lies.

There is an old saying that goes something like, "If you meet Buddha on the path, kill him." This is because you can never be *that* Buddha. So, be inspired by that Buddha, but don't try to imitate him. You will get nowhere with imitation. You have to follow your own path and be authentic. That is the way to spiritual progress and attainment.

Sunday, 17 November 2013:

Some of the best advice Dr. Kundan Singh from my doctoral program ever gave me was "to surrender." This is not so easy for Westerners. There may be thoughts that the person to whom we surrender will take advantage of us. Well, I suppose this is like love. We have to love fully to really experience love. If we withhold our love, calculate, hedge our bets, we do not really experience love.

To love fully, we have to be open to the possibility of being utterly crushed and destroyed. That is the sacrifice that is needed. But when we surrender fully to the cosmos, to nature, to the Mother, we know that She will always carry us in Her arms, nurture us, take care of us, and She will never let anything bad happen to us. I know that this may sound "out there," but it is the Truth.

One of Santa Muerte's many forms

Friday, 1 August 2014:

I was in Barrio Tepito yesterday afternoon to hand out recruitment flyers at the monthly Santa Muerte feast day. I passed out three hundred flyers; this could have been easily a thousand flyers. Although the November first feast day is Her big day, there were many in attendance yesterday.

I heard someone speaking bad gringo Spanish, asking someone, "Is this a Catholic belief?" I quickly moved on. For years, I have been the only white person at these feasts. It's not that I want to keep this to myself. It's just that white Westerners very often appropriate and ruin things.

The gringo caught up to me, and began asking me questions. I quickly realized that this was R. Andrew Chestnut, the guy who wrote the only Santa Muerte book in English…published during my time at ITP by Oxford University Press.

I thought the book was rather weak and prejudiced; it's written by an outsider who barely speaks Spanish. He asked if he could interview me. I said, "Well, I'm doing my own study," and handed him a flyer. "I am busy with this now, but the flyer has my contact info," I told him.

He was accompanied by a Mexican woman, who was his photographer and translator. I am unsure how to feel about this. I imagine that my interview would be beneficial for him. However, I doubt that there is anything that I could gain from interviewing him. He's not a devotee, so he doesn't even meet the criterion for my study.

Later tonight, I got into a fight with my wife. This is a fight we have often: theory versus practice. She is the theory side, and I, the practice side. It's not that I am opposed to theory; it's just that once I read about something, I have to experience it for myself. This is part of my Tantric path (and my practice of psychotherapy): theory is meaningless without practical realization.

She would prefer to read books and imagine the world outside. And she is unhappy about me fraternizing with shirtless men covered with tattoos, prostitutes, and transvestites at a Santa Muerte feast in Barrio Tepito.

Coming out of the Tepito metro station, I take a wrong turn. I have never been to the Middle East, by I suspect that souks or bazaars there are similar to the *tianguis* of Tepito. It is vast, and one can lose their way quickly. The entrance to the metro is totally obscured by *puestos*, vendor stalls selling everything from computers to clothing to Chinese cigarettes. I know my way, but even I get turned around sometimes inside the *tianguis*.

Walking on the sidewalk, there is shade provided by tarpaulins overhead, but the traffic barely moves. Old people hobble along; fat people stop to look at a prospective purchase; couples make out; groups of people walk five abreast, forming an impassable wall. Moving onto the street is little better. Cars move slowly through the crowds, in opposite directions, causing jams; men on scooters and motorcycles, often with several family members on board or carrying a baby under an arm, snake through in fits and starts; men move merchandise with overloaded dollies, called here *diablitos* or little devils; and the sun overhead is powerful.

Sunday, 10 August 2014:

Since Passing out 300 flyers at the Santa Muerte feast, I have received no responses. I can see that people have been to my website, because of the counter, but no one has contacted me. I am a little surprised by this, but I am not worried.

One of the ways that Mexico is very different than the US is that the written word does not carry as much weight as the spoken word. I know this seems strange. It seems that the written word is often not trusted, and is often ignored.

It may be that I will have to approach devotees individually, and try to recruit that way. I don't relish the idea, but I am sure that it will lend richness to the study. I can also approach a couple of people who are respected in the community. I am sure that they will grant me interviews, and they may also be of help in recruiting other participants. Meanwhile, I am pretty immersed in the study, and I am writing every day.

The neighborhood that is the epicenter of the Santa Muerte cult is called Barrio Bravo de Tepito. *Bravo* means *fierce*. This is where Americans got the word *brave* to signify an Indian warrior. So, *brave* in this sense, does not mean *brave* as in English which is *valiente* in Spanish, but *fierce*.

Saturday, 16 August 2014:

I had a flash of fear during meditation. Thinking of my dissertation and life in general, there is a lot of mediation on death. I went off thinking about the future. I lost faith and saw myself as old and infirm. A patient recently was shocked that I don't have health insurance. Thinking back, I have never needed insurance. Insurance is a racket. One has insurance "just in case," but that case seldom comes. This is why insurance companies are so rich. I trust in God. I didn't tell the patient that. It's usually best to say less about yourself as a therapist. I try to show that doing what most people do is often a bad idea. There are no guarantees when following the herd. One should act on instinct and intuition, trusting in God. There are ups and downs, as there have to be in a dualistic world, but everything works out perfectly.

Tuesday, 26 August 2014:

This morning, there was a huge moth on the ceiling of my office, the size of a small bat or bird (6" wings). I watched it. It had beautiful and intricate gray and black designs on its wings. Mexicans take these huge, dark moths to be a sign of death. I saw the moth as a sign that Santa Muerte had heard my prayers. I got a plastic bag from the kitchen and captured the moth to release it outside. I tried to get a closer to better look at it, but it struggled and flew away.

Tuesday, 9 September 2014:

I went to the Santa Muerte shrine in Tepito today to seek an interview with Doña Queta (Enriqueta Romero). The sun was very hot. I am not a huge fan of walking around this area. Wearing a shirt and tie, I got a lot of looks. I get looks anyway, as I am a tall white guy with a big red beard and thick-framed glasses.

When I approached the shrine complex—the complex is on the first floor of a several story apartment building. In front, in the street, are hundreds of flower bouquets. On the left side is a little stall selling Santa Muerte paraphernalia. To the right is the shrine itself, and to the right of the shrine is a *velatorio*, or candle room—there was a small white dog in front that I played with for a bit. He was very sweet. I learned that his name is Poseidon. After I purchased two white candles in glass tubes with Santa Muerte's image, I was approached by a little black cat who was also very loving. His name is Negro, appropriately.

I knelt and prayed to Santa Muerte to help me in this dissertation work. I felt an intense shaking. Quite frightened and thinking that there was an earthquake, I looked around me. People stood chatting or walking by in the street. There was no earthquake, at least not outside, at least none that others perceived. I am unsure what happened, if it was my nervousness or what. Was this a sign? Was Santa Muerte communicating with me? I have learned that it is best not to rush to explain or define these experiences; naming tends to destroy or, at least, to limit.

I approached the old man, Raimundo, in the paraphernalia stall, and asked if Doña Queta was available. He told me that she was out. I introduced myself and told him about the study that I am conducting. I told him that I am a devotee, and showed him my tattoo for proof. I told him that I have been working as a volunteer at the community mental health clinic for years. I told him that I know Doña

Queta, but that we hadn't spoken for a few years. He seemed interested in the work I am doing. Of all the times that I have visited the shrine, this was the first time that he was polite and friendly to me.

When I approached, he was painting a small white Santa Muerte statue that resembled *La Catrina*. I made arrangements to return on the 23rd to talk to Doña Queta. I think that it is important to interview her first, so that she blesses the work that I am doing, and can provide me with other participants. Without Doña Queta, many of us would probably not know of Santa Muerte.

Tuesday, 23 September 2014:

After a week in Guatemala, I returned to the Santa Muerte shrine in Tepito today. Doña Queta was sitting in the store gluing strings of pearls to statues of *La Catrina*, the iconic rich-lady skeleton of Day of the Dead. I explained to her what it is that I am doing with the study. I bought a couple of white candles. I placed one at the altar, along with a cigarette, and took the other home. I prayed to Santa Muerte to help me with this work.

I explained to Doña Queta how my study will differ from that of Andrew Chesnutt's, in that I am a devotee and want to tell my story and the stories of other devotees.

She was not happy about Chesnutt's book, *Devoted to Death*. She said that he wrote *pendejadas* (bullshit) and lies. I said that I had seen him in the street asking people questions without a recorder. I said, "And he just trusts all of this to his memory?" "Who needs memories if you write lies," she responded, shrugging her shoulders. "It's for this reason that I need to record the interviews."

I explained that there are rules for doing a research study that must be followed. I was already working on this dissertation when Chesnutt's book was published. I am not interested to know which parts of his book Doña Queta found objectionable. However, it does not speak well of a researcher when his participants feel the way that Doña Queta feels.

Doña Queta was very friendly. She said that she couldn't do an interview until her husband, Raimundo, returned to watch the shop. During this time her daughter, who runs a cleaning products *puesto* across the street and up the block, came to ask Doña Queta to watch her *puesto*. Doña Queta asked me to watch her store, and went up the street for a while.

I felt honored. I played with her little white dog, Poseidon, people came to pray or to make offerings at the shrine, but no one came to buy anything until Doña Queta returned. I noticed that I had smoked many cigarettes while there, and had not seen Doña Queta smoke. I remember her smoking the last times that we talked in 2009. She said that she had cancer, lost a lung, and so had to quit smoking. She asked why I thought she got cancer while I am healthy. I shrugged and suggested that it's genetics. She countered that it was stress.

There were red and golden apples left as offerings to Santa Muerte. When street people passed by, Doña Queta gave the apples to them to eat as *prasad*, and they would sort of genuflect with gratitude.

While we were talking, a young gay man with beached white hair approached. He started to go into what Doña Queta figured would be a long story. She stopped him, saying, "Yes, yes! What do you need?" He told her that his Santa Muerte statue had fallen and broken, and he wanted to know if they do repairs. "No. We don't." She smiled at him. Tepiteños are no-bullshit people.

Speaking about belief and practice, Doña Queta said that for her the most important thing is faith. I told her that I am not a Catholic, but a Hindu. She asked, "How many gods are there?" I said, "One." She said, "Exactly! There are many names and many forms of the one God. It doesn't matter what you call it."

She said that two of her sons are in prison, and that she has no use for the police or the government, and I agreed. We both agreed that voting is useless, never a real choice.

After hanging around and chatting for two hours, her husband hadn't returned, we made a date to do the interview at 12pm on Thursday. She said she would take me upstairs and show me her personal altar.

Devotees would arrive on a motor scooter, park in front, buy some candles, and proceed to the shrine. Poseidon would walk over and pee on their bikes. This was while I was not rubbing his belly and scratching him.

Thursday, 25 September 2014:

I was back at the Tepito shrine today to interview Doña Queta. Again, I bought two white candles, one for the shrine and the other to take home. I knelt and prayed that the work go well. I offered the candle and a cigarette, as usual.

Doña Queta was very welcoming and hospitable to me. She took me upstairs and showed me two small rooms, one containing her personal Santa Muerte altar, the other her separate *Santería* altar. Except for the size and quantity of paraphernalia, the altar looked more or less like mine and others I have seen. I brought her a black clay skull from Oaxaca as a present. She was excited, kissing it many times. She placed the skull among many others in her Santa Muerte altar. There were many unique figures, including some of San Simón (Maximón). She did not want me to photograph the altar, and I complied.

We went into a second floor room to do the interview, and she would not let me record. She wanted to know the questions first. So, we did a sort of practice run until she felt comfortable.

Then, she let me record as I asked the questions again. This was a good idea from someone who has been interviewed many times. It's better to have good, solid answers than to fumble around and forget to say something important. She did not want to sign the consent form. She asked me to read it to her, as she made a point that she is not an educated person. She got tired of my long reading, and just said that she gives her consent, that she trusts me. I am sure that this is something that will come up often in this study. Mexicans tend to privilege the spoken word over the written. There seems to be mistrust of the written word, and of signing things.

The interview went very well. Doña Queta came across to me as very humble. She stressed love, humility, and faith. Her position to Santa Muerte seems to me like *bhakti*, loving devotion. Her wants or needs are simple; she wants to live life fully and happily.

After the interview, we sat in the *tiendita* downstairs by the shrine as she worked on statues of *La Catrina*. My wife likes *La Catrina*, so I asked how much the statues cost. She said that they are not for sale, that she makes them for Santa Muerte for Her November 1 feast day. After that, she says that she gives them to others. She said that she will give me one, and I thanked her.

We talked about David Romo's Santa Muerte Church. She has a rather low opinion of him, saying that he talks too much. Talking about Romo changing the image of Santa Muerte to the Angle of Death (a white female angel), she said that this is what his wife looks like. I said that I had read that he is in prison for being part of a gang of kidnappers, and that I doubted the charges as he was a very vocal opponent of the government. She laughed, and said, "He's on vacation." She confirmed that he was part of the gang, that he would arrange the ransoms paid by family members of victims.

Speaking of Hermano Parka and Yamarash in Ecatepec, she said that they are *buena onda* (cool). I told her that her opinions of these various people in the Santa Muerte community confirmed my own intuitions.

She asked me if I know Alfonso Hernandez. I did not. Apparently, he is responsible for the Santa Muerte shrine at Peralvillo and Matamoros. I recognized this from one of the anonymous Santa Muerte books in my bibliography. She gave me a flyer for a book presentation in Galeria Peralvillo on Tuesday the 30th. The book is an anthropological study of Santeria. She said that she will be there, that I should come, and she will introduce me to Alfonso Hernandez who is also *buena onda.*

I am really excited. Things are progressing nicely. I spent a lot of time sitting on the stool in the *tiendita*, answering questions from customers. I felt at peace.

Sunday, 28 September 2014:

I have been sick with cold/flu since coming back from Guatemala. I have not been getting the bed rest that I need in order to get well. I have not been doing my regular *sadhana* since before I left. I find myself chanting the Ganesha mantra unintentionally. I light incense and recite mantras as usual, but I have not been doing full *puja*. I am lighting more candles and incense and praying to Santa Muerte more than usual.

Monday, 29 September 2014:

It is almost October and it is still raining every afternoon. The clouds overhead tumble past like big sacks of dirty laundry. It is my theory that the rain combines with the air pollution to create the hale that falls every other time it rains.

Tomorrow, I work at the clinic in Tepito. Afterwards, I am to meet Doña Queta in Colonia Peralvillo for a book presentation about

Santería. *Santería* does not specifically interest me, and I am not treating it in the dissertation study because it is an Afro-Cuban phenomenon that is rather foreign to Mexico with its almost non-existent black population. I am interested to see the area, the Santa Muerte shrine, and the man who maintains it, Alfonso Hernandez.

I lit a candle and did a little ritual this morning to ask Santa Muerte to help me to get at least one interview per week. This is my intention.

Recently, near the Santa Muerte shrine in Tepito, a street person approached me speaking loudly. He asked how to get to La Villa where sits the Basilica to the Virgin of Guadalupe. I thought for a moment before telling him to walk north on Calle Imprenta. I said that I always see the *guadalupanos* (devotees of Guadalupe) taking that route during the annual pilgrimage in December. He began yelling that he is a *guadalupano*. He thanked me. Walking away, I was surprised that I have been here so long that I could give directions to this man. I've never been to the basilica myself.

Tuesday, 30 September 2014:

I realize that elements of my *sadhana*, doing rituals to accomplish an end, are pretty much the same as the intention-setting exercises in Anderson and Braud's books.

After seeing patients at the clinic in Tepito today, I went to the Santa Muerte shrine. I bought two white candles, as usual (one for the shrine and one for the home altar), talked with Ray a little, petted the cats and dogs, and waited my turn to make the offering of candle and cigarette. I knelt and asked Santa Muerte to help me with this work, to send devotee participants to me. I have often noticed the reflective quality of the glass in front of the figure of Santa Muerte; it is easy to see everything behind you when facing Her.

I took the train from Tepito to Garibaldi and then walked to Colonia Peralvillo for the book presentation. The talk was boring for me. Mexican academics, like Mexican politicians, when asked a yes or no question go on for half an hour until you have forgotten the question and no longer care for an answer. Doña Queta and her two daughters were happy to see me. Doña Queta introduced me to Alfonso Hernandez, who is the director of cultural patrimony for Delegación Cuauhtémoc. He was friendly, and said that he is willing to be interviewed. There was too much handshaking and photo-ops for a longer conversation. He gave me his card.

Tuesday, 7 October 2014:

Throughout this project, I have pretty consistently kept a white candle burning in my Santa Muerte altar. I am reminded of the old Fritz Lang film *Der müde Tod* (1921) (*The Weary Death*, usually translated as *Destiny*) where Death has a chamber filled with tall, white candles, each one representing a person's life.

I sometimes become frustrated with the Spanish language (I should say Mexican language, as Mexico is the largest Spanish-speaking country, and has a language that differs greatly from that of Spain.) because it has so few words. There are so many words in English. There are words to express so many nuances that Spanish lacks. If the English language is a razor, Spanish is a club.

People have countered, "I thought that Latin peoples were emotional and expressive." My answer is that they are so because they lack the words, the symbols, the stand-ins for direct experience, what Lacan would call the Real. Language is an abstraction, a distancing from the Real. The more words we have in English, the less we have to feel. Instead, we English-speakers can think, describe, talk about, and abstract ourselves away from what is real. The Spanish-speaker is thusly closer to the actual experience of the Real. Language is built on opposition. Every word carries within it its polar opposite; there is no other way. Because of this, one pole tends to be preferred over the other. But inside this abstracted concept of reality, it is impossible for one to exist without the other. There is no day without night, no life without death…and so on.

I went to the Tepito shrine today after work at the clinic. I bought four white candles. Ray wrapped the three that I was taking home in newspaper. Doña Queta arrived, and called me, "*mi amigo.*" Ray took a photo of us in front of Santa Muerte wearing a sparkly pink dress.

The author with Doña Queta at the Tepito shrine

Doña Queta cleaning shrine

Thursday, 9 October 2014:

Yesterday, I met with Alfonso Hernandez in his office in the Cuauhtémoc delegation building near Metro Buenavista.

I'm on the street, ahead of time, but I can't find the delegation building. I circle several blocks, and begin to perspire. I finally call the number on the card I was given. A secretary answers. I have a hard time hearing because of the traffic. I keep repeating the cross streets where I am standing, hoping that I am making myself understood.

After a while, an aged and portly uniformed policeman approaches me and asks, "Señor Primavera?" He has been sent to lead me to the delegation building. We walk for several blocks, chatting as we go. The building is a huge, modern concrete monstrosity from the 70s, occupying an entire block. The policeman bypasses security and leads me to an elevator and up to a suite of open offices of concrete and glass.

A secretary leads me into Alfonso's big, airy office that is cluttered with stacks of papers and files and Aztec artefacts. She hands some forms to Alfonso, who glances over them before carefully removing a fancy fountain pen from his desk and signing. Other women move about the space, talking and passing papers back and forth.

Apparently, Alfonso's office is responsible for the iconic Angel of Independence monument that occupies the center of a roundabout in the Paseo de la Reforma. This abundance of bureaucracy reminded me of the Mexican immigration office where often I've stood in line for three hours in order to find out which line I need to stand in next. My conversation with Alfonso was continually interrupted by women needing his signature on a form or his comment on this or that.

Alfonso is not what Mexicans would think of as a typical Santa Muerte devotee. He is a great grandfather, college educated, and a government bureaucrat. He name drops Walter Benjamin, and his take on Santa Muerte is rather intellectual and considered. He told me that he was born in Tepito and that the people of Tepito and their customs have been an interest for him since the 1970s. I am not the first researcher to interview Alfonso. He tells me that people from Italy, Germany, and Switzerland have come before. He mentions, like Queta before him, that Andrew Chestnut is the worst, and that he hopes that I being a devotee will make me honest.

Alfonso was raised Catholic, but relates more to Mexican pre-Hispanic spirituality. He stresses the abuses of the Spanish, that Catholicism was forced upon them, and that Tepito was the last area of what is now Mexico City to fall to the Spanish.

He tells me, "I've read Walter Benjamin's famous essay about how moderns are more and more distancing their selves from death. Death now happens in hospitals rather than in the home. For Mexicans, death is another form of life. We exist, made of cosmic dust; we have to transcend. For this reason, the *calaveras* of Posada are interesting; dead people eating beans and tortillas, doing very daily, quotidian Mexican things. There's a cycle of life and death of the body, like there is day and night. This duality, day/night, black/white all go together. I don't think darkness is bad."

Saturday, 11 October 2014:

There are currently eggplants placed as offerings in the shrine of Santa Muerte. I am thinking of asking Doña Queta if I can take them after the anniversary on the 31st and cook something with them. We could then consume the food as *prasad*, imbued with Santa Muerte's blessing.

Monday, 27 October 2014:

I've been feeling badly since returning from Guatemala. I am not sure what happened. I feel tired all the time. My *sadhana* has been suspended for some time. I began a cleanse diet and some light exercise. I am feeling a bit more energetic. I need to return to my usual *sadhana*, but I don't feel that I'm there yet. The Santa Muerte feast and Halloween are on Friday. I feel weary. I need to make some recruitment flyers, but I am still unsure on the approach.

Saturday, 1 November 2014:

Today is the first day of the Days of the Dead. I have been fasting for a week. The first three days I ate only a spicy soup of green mung beans. The next three days I consumed only liquids. I became very weak and faint at times. I walked a great distance on the first day of liquid-only and I felt like I might die. All of this tended to prepare me for the Santa Muerte feast on Friday in Tepito. I had been thinking a lot about what language to use for recruitment flyers. While lying in bed in a state of terrible weakness the idea came to me.

My wife set up the *ofrenda* in our living room on Thursday. I was too weak to help her, but we both carved pumpkins. Today, I did my bit outside, making a path of candles, *cempasuchiles* (marigolds), and *pata de leon*. I put out an incense burner with charcoal to burn copal. On the *ofrenda*, I placed a photo of Jacky, a can of beer, a joint, a glass of water, three white candles, some food, and cigarettes.

Monday, 3 November 2014:

I feel that my life is perfect and really could not get any better. Then I am frozen with fear at the thought of it all disappearing. The last time that I remember being completely and unashamedly happy and surrendered myself completely, a big earthquake hit. I am afraid that if I relax my position that something awful will happen. I think, "If I keep all my muscles tensed, then nothing bad will happen; or if it does, I will be prepared." If things are really good they must necessarily become very bad. This is the eternal play of the Mother in her dance of manifestation and dissolution. What goes up must come down, and if I feel great, feeling lousy is bound to follow, and vice versa.

I have PTSD symptoms, many of them. I have PTSD and Mexicans don't get it. They don't understand me feeling unhinged and disturbed. They grew up with earthquakes. I did not. People have called me *puto* (faggot) because of this. This a quantity over quality thing again. It does not matter whether there is death or destruction caused by the quake. The earth moves violently and all stability is lost. What you thought was stable and lasting is unstable and fleeting. It is a horrible fucking feeling. And I cannot shake it. I constantly think that an earthquake is happening when it isn't. There is hardly a way to tell. I put a glass of water out to see if the water moved. It didn't.

I hanged a pendulum from the ceiling. Maybe that will let me know. Because once this happens to you, it feels like it keeps happening.

Of course, I am not in control of earthquakes or death. Trying to remain in a state of equipoise is not easy. To see success and failure, life and death as equal takes some work; or it takes letting go of working, of striving. Fearing the highs because of their attendant lows is no way to live. Life and death are both wrapped up in every single moment.

Patients often ask why they cannot be happy all the time. The obvious answer is that if they were happy all the time, they would not know the difference between happy and sad. It is only by contrast that light stands apart from the dark.

Walking to the Tepito shrine, I pass along Avenida del Trabajo (Avenue of Work, such a grim, honest name). It always seems to be hot in Tepito. The sun beats down and there are few shade trees. The other side of the street is piled with trash. I pass the triangle of a green area where homeless people live. There is a makeshift Santa Muerte altar by a tree. *Activos* (people who inhale solvents) mill about like zombies. There is a pedestrian bridge overhead leading to the Tepito Metro station; its sign with its boxing glove symbol is visible. I pass a large walled-in area where shirtless men and boys play handball. The smell of pot smoke is always present. Across the street there is a hand-written sign advertising liver tacos. The heat and the smell of viscera make my stomach turn. I step off the sidewalk and am almost hit by a turning motor scooter ridden by a boy and a girl holding a baby in her arms.

Death is always all around us, even moreso in Mexico. My wife has been very upset over a recent incident where a number of students were kidnapped, tortured, and killed in the state of Guerrero. As I typically avoid the media, I do not hear about every atrocity that occurs. However, I recently read of the massacres in the state of Tamaulipas that took place in 2011, while I was living here.

Apparently, Los Zetas cartel were stopping buses and selecting passengers. They would take the passengers and make them fight one another, gladiator-style, to the death. The "winner" would then be sent on a suicide mission as a hit man. How does one go on under such circumstances?

Thursday, 6 November 2014:

I am impressed that when I ask participants about the frequency that they think of death, they invariably say, "All the time." In the West, the topic of death is avoided strongly.

Tuesday, 11 November 2014:

At the last Santa Muerte feast in Tepito, I was approached by a gothic couple. I stand out in the crowd, so, Araceli, the female, asked if she could take a photo with me. I agreed, and they agreed to participate in my study.

Araceli and the author in Tepito

Today Araceli and Juan came to the clinic in Tepito to be interviewed. I first spoke with Juan, and he told me the following story.

"Santa Muerte has protected me for ten years. I am a widower. Before, I didn't like these things, death and all of that. Though, these things always drew my attention, skeletons and skulls. My current wife, Araceli, had skulls on her belt and necklace when I met her. There was this accident and nothing happened to me. My wife and daughter died on the highway. I was driving. We went into a ravine. Sadly, they both died. The doctors said they died instantly and didn't suffer. I just had superficial wounds. How? I don't know. Why? I don't know." He shakes his head slowly. "Lots of people said it was because of *La Muerte* that I wasn't dead."

"I had a streak of using drugs and alcohol in the streets of Mexico City. I was drinking with street people. My mom looked for me and helped me to gain strength. I started working in Mexico. I had been living in the state of Hidalgo. I was never so stable until I met my current wife, Araceli."

"I was working, trying to stabilize, and I met an old friend. He told me that *La Niña* protected me." He makes a look of disbelief. "Me? Why? Help me to understand. I didn't believe or understand him. He told me about the religion, that she helped me and blessed me. He said, "The *Niña Blanca* protected you." I said, "What *niña?*" I thought he was talking about my daughter. He said, "No, friend," and he showed me his necklace with this pendant of Death, and said, "This is my saint. She's the one who protected you." I said, "No. I don't need these things." He told me that I should quickly get a small yellow figure of her and ask her. "But ask her with confidence." I said, "You're crazy, friend! I don't buy that crap!" He shakes his head.

"Three months later, I had a problem with the bank. I made a deposit in Bancomer, and they took all my money. I asked the girl why and she said that I had a debt of $20,000 pesos." He looks surprised. "That's not possible. They locked my account; I couldn't get my money. This went on for months. I asked help from saint after saint. I went to Mercado Sonora and bought a little yellow Santa Muerte statue. I put her in my house and, with faith, asked her a favor. About a month later, the bank called me. They asked me to come and sign a document, and claim my money. They told me that they had made a mistake. There was another guy in the same municipality with the exact same name and same birth date. They made me take a polygraph and they checked my signature."

"After that, I went to the shrine in Tepito to give thanks. I've been going every month on the first since then. I hand out candy to the other devotees. It's been two years. Family members hear my story and see my Santa Muerte pendant, and they say, "Give me one!""

"I don't know what happened, but she helped me. And I always have her image with me. I put up a little altar in a corner of my house. I no longer keep my money in the bank, but at the altar. There, I know it's protected."

"I don't understand a lot of things, but I know that life begins to end in death. No one is immortal. She's an emanation of the Creator. She's not something satanic, like the devil or something. But everything, including the devil, is a creation of Our Father God. The devil was the most beautiful angel. He rebelled and was sent to hell. He wanted to be God, and so was sent below. This is my experience with Santa Muerte. Believing in Santa Muerte has brought me many blessings, health, and a lot of work, thanks to God and *la Niña Blanca*."

"She says what I can and can't do. I'm working and I hurt my foot. I say, "Help me," the crap goes away, and I continue on. I'm lost, I can't find the place; I've lost the telephone number. I ask Her, and I am no longer lost. She guides me. When I don't know the way, she knocks." He knocks on the table. "And She says, "Not that way, this way.""

"Where I live, there's lots of crime. But my wife and I feel safe, because we know she's protecting us. If they're going to rob you, they'll ask for the time or for a light for their cigarette. If they come that close, they can see my Santa Muerte pendant. They respect that, and they leave me alone. Lots of people here and where I live believe in her or, at least, respect her."

"Everything that begins ends. Death is another beginning. Santa Muerte comes to collect you to bring you before the Boss. The incarnate body begins a new life, because it decomposes and is fed on by germs, insects, etc., in the earth. The spirit, the soul, goes to God, assisted by Santa Muerte. Santa Muerte is for us, the faithful, and death is for the rest."

"I don't fear death. We all live to die. This is a very illogical contradiction. Why do we live to die? You live, you reproduce, get to know people, live a good life, but in the end you're going to die. You live to die. Many people say, "I don't understand your logic." This is the logic of devotees. Life is in death, and in death there is life. This is the cycle of life. When you die and are in the earth, you're fed on by insects and you give life to them and to plants that give life to others. Those insects reproduce. The trees grow, produce fruit, you consume that fruit, and it passes back to the earth like everything."

I was quite moved and impressed by Juan's story and his deep understanding.

Wednesday, 12 November 2014:

Losing someone you love is terribly hard until you realize that death goes hand in hand with life, that the two cannot exist in isolation.

Our male cat has been sick for a while, vomiting and eating very little. He threw up in the bed last night. When I returned from work today, he had vomited all over my wife's office. I found him hiding under an armoire, a place he never goes.

I thought of outdoor cats I had as a child that would wander off when it was their time to die. He was so weak that he didn't protest when I pulled him out by his tail. I hugged and cuddled him. I gave him a good brushing, to see if he would protest when I brushed his tail as he typically does. He was very limp and acquiescent.

I took him to the veterinary hospital a few blocks away. The vet said that he is at least fifteen years old, nearly twice the age we were told by a previous vet, and around the upper limits of a cat's life. He was admitted, and they are going to rehydrate him and run blood tests. I couldn't help tearing up in the examination room. Maybe it had something to do with the vet's caring manner. I don't know. I love this cat so much.

I inherited this cat through my wife. She adopted him from a shelter, and his health has always been shaky. He has benign tumors growing on his upper eyelids and he is always snotty. A vet commented in the past that he has the face of a boxer. I used to be rather indifferent to him, but once I fell into his web I was held fast by his charms. I recognized in the moment of coming to love this cat that this was attachment, a *klesha* that will lead to pain.

I realize that this may be his time to die. I am more or less alright with that. The main thing is that I do not want him to suffer unnecessarily. I do not want him to go on for my benefit.

Monday, 17 November 2014:

Taji, the cat, seems little better or worse for having been in the hospital for five nights. I washed his cat bed and sheets, and brought it to the hospital for him to sleep in. He seems to like that. The hospital is noisy. The dogs bark a lot, especially when people enter and exit.

A woman that works there takes the dogs for walks, always during the visiting hours. She seems clumsy and overly present. If she is not taking the dogs, she is moving something else, dropping it, slamming doors, etc. However, she is very friendly and attentive. She seems to be in tune with what is going on with Taji. He sometimes eats the ground beef we bring. It's always his choice, as at home. Since he does not show that much interest in the meat, I feed it to an abandoned cat that looks similar to him, though only six months old, who is in the cubicle next to Tajin. I also feed it to a three-month-old kitten that has had a spinal injury, and cannot move its hind quarter. That kitten is filled with life. She moves around rapidly on her two good legs, and does not seem to understand that she is disabled.

Taji rests in his cat bed, like he typically does. He spends most of his time sleeping, and all he cares about is a meat snack or sleeping next to my wife at night.

I have learned so much from this cat. He taught me a great deal about *bhakti*, loving devotion. He lavishes love on my wife. She is the one who saved him when all the vets said that he would not survive. By all accounts, he should not have lived this long. He was rescued from the streets where he was depleted physically and beaten. He is always loyal and thankful to her, even if it is I who feeds him by hand and takes him to the hospital when he's sick.

This cat and I have had to spend a lot of time together without my wife. We were sort of forced together. I used to go to my wife's apartment to do laundry before we lived together. There were times when she was out of the country, and I came to feel a closeness to him. I made up songs to sing to him. He and I passed the time together that we both shared apart from my wife.

His health never seemed good. I made the joke that he was a Frankenstein cat made up of parts of other cats. When we had to take in my wife's mother's girl cats, he was enamored of them. They were beautiful angora sisters, though also adopted from the street. Even though they were all fixed, they would have next to nothing to do with Taji. They acted violently towards him.

Thinking back to a little over a year ago, when Taji was very sick and My wife brought up the idea of him dying or the possibility of having him euthanized, my mind is different now. At that time, I knew that he still had life to live. So, I did a little ritual. I performed mantras and mudras, and I gave him a portion of my Shakti, my power or life-force. He got up immediately and began to eat on his own. He has been is good health since that time.

Now that I learn that he is fifteen years old (reaching the upper limits for a cat), and considering his general state, I do not want to keep him alive artificially. I want him to die when it's time for him to die.

I know that this sounds strange, but I have found that communicating with him telepathically (forming thoughts, intentions, etc., in my head, and focusing them at him) has worked much more effectively than using human words. This has worked so well that, at times, he gets angry and walks away when it is something that he does not agree with. By this same method, I have advised him of his current state, and that he might die. I have even gone as far as to communicate that he is very old and that he may not live a decent life much longer, and that we may have to kill him. He has seemed quite reasonable and accepting of his situation. I have told him that he is an angel, a being of light, filled with compassion. When he dies (leaves his current body), he will transmigrate to a human body. I know this because of his karma. If he does not transmigrate or reincarnate as a human, he will go straight to the abode of Shiva, Shakti, and Ganesha on Mount Kailasha. He seems indifferent.

Tuesday, 18 November 2014:

The community mental health clinic where I work in Barrio Tepito is on a street filled with pet and aquarium supply vendors. Directly outside the door of the clinic men work from the trunk of a car, filling plastic bags with blue, treated water and fish to be sold. Once the right amount of fish has been scooped into a bag, it is inflated with air, and placed in line with other similar bags lining the wall of the clinic. Overhead in a lone, skinny tree, blue-black *zanates* (black birds or grackles) with straight, sharp beaks pace back and forth. When some of the little fish fall into the gutter, the *zanates* swoop down to eat them. For years, I have stood on the sidewalk watching this hunting display which is a rather odd sight in a city.

Saturday, 22 November 2014:

Walking to the shrine in Tepito on Wednesday, I had to step out of the way of a procession of *guadalupanos* (devotees of the Virgin of Guadalupe) on their way to the basilica. They carried banners and an image of the virgin, and a small marching band played at the head of a line of several hundred people. This is not an uncommon sight in this area, as it is on the way to the basilica. Typically though, they are more numerous around the 12th of December, Guadalupe's feast day. I thought of a similar scene in *Batalla en el Cielo* (*Battle in Heaven*), a film by Mexican filmmaker Carlos Reygadas, where an on looker, when watching a similar procession of *guadalupanos*, says critically, "Puros borregos," (pure sheep).

At the shrine, Queta greeted me enthusiastically, kissing on the cheek. I told her about my cat having to be hospitalized, and she was very sympathetic. I said that I had asked Santa Muerte to take him if it was his time, just not to let him suffer. Queta commended my prayer, saying that we all go sometime. Queta's friendly presence and being at the shrine made me feel nice and at ease.

Many people were lined up to take their turns praying before the image of Santa Muerte. I overheard a man who was kneeling before the image crying and praying for someone who had died in a loud, pleading voice. Because of this and the many people buying candles, I thought it time to take my leave. I felt that what I was witnessing was private and deserved respectful ignorance. I forget that there are differences between Mexican and American notions of what is private.

Tuesday, 25 November 2014:

"Without the awareness of death everything is ordinary, trivial. It is only because death is stalking us that the world is an unfathomable mystery."—Don Juan, *Tales of Power*

"Without an awareness of the presence of our death, there is no power, no mystery."—Don Juan, *Tales of Power*

Monday, 1 December 2014:

To talk about syncretism seems superfluous, as pretty much every spiritual or religious tradition is an amalgamation of previous traditions; Judaism, Christianity, and Islam are foremost in this line. Whether we are of European decent, Arab, Mexican, et al, we were all once "indigenous," with our own spiritual traditions that were trampled over and syncretized to accord with monotheism.

Friday, 5 December 2014:

Being on death watch is somewhat exhausting. In the past when friends or relatives have died, it has always been sudden; I would get the news later. This is the first time that I have actively waited for one to die. I know that it's coming. The thing is that She comes for us all, and I don't usually think much about it.

I already feel gaps in his presence. When he was in the hospital, I often stood in the kitchen and thought that I heard him sniffling behind me, looking for a snack. I would turn and he would not be there.

Truthfully, this cat has been a consistent pain in the ass. He has always required much more care and attention than the other two cats. It is often difficult to get him to eat. He prefers raw ground beef, but the vet said that this is bad for his kidneys. It is typical that we offer him a cat buffet of four types of food from which to choose, including pureed tuna. Not only is this not enough, he wants to be fed by hand.

He often vomits on the bed, especially if the sheets have just been changed; he vomits on the carpet, anywhere but the easy-to-clean tile floors that cover this house. As annoying as he can be, and he requires a lot of patience, he is a definite presence. When he is not here, I feel his absence.

I couldn't find him for a few hours today, and I felt a slight panic. I found a puddle of vomit under a wardrobe in my wife's office. I got a flashlight and looked underneath; he wasn't there. I cleaned up the vomit. I was worried that he would go to some difficult to reach hiding place to die. He had done this when he was very sick, before I took him to the hospital. When I was a child, our indoor-outdoor cats would wander off to die in the woods. This is one of those painful facts of life that our mother explained to us when we were quite young, that when cats are ready to die they simply wander away.

When Jacky and I were in high school, he sent me a cassette tape of music that he had made and recorded in his bedroom in his dad's mobile home in Texas. He mailed the cassette to me during a summer that I was spending at my father's in Tennessee. The cassette had a hand-painted cover that Jacky had made. He wanted me to listen to the tape and send it back, with the stipulation that I not make a copy of it. This was typical of Jacky. So much of his work is now lost to the world because he would not let me make a duplicate of it. The music was incredibly good, and I listened to the tape often. Some of the lyrics of two of the songs are still very much with me. One lyric was, "I just want to dissolve in her and never leave." Another was, "A big bang and the world is gone. Be happy; things last too long." It strikes me now that these lyrics have a deep esoteric meaning that Jacky did not necessarily intend. But who knows? There are so many things that happen this way. Who is to say what unseen force is taking a hand?

I also remember a time in high school when Jacky wanted our friend Melynda to do something. She began, "I can't, because I have to…" Jacky stopped her there, and said, "Have to. The only thing you *have* to do is die." The absolute truth, and very prophetic.

112

Saturday, 6 December 2014:

Like with the earthquakes, Taji's illness reminds me that death is always near us, sometimes closer, sometimes farther away. Last night death could be felt in the room, hovering.

Sunday, 7 December 2014:

Taji has left his cat body for Mount Kailasha, the Himalayan abode of Shiva, Parvati, and Ganesha.

He was in a bad way yesterday, vomiting green bile, and my wife and I went to the veterinary hospital to ask about putting him to sleep. They were really busy, and we couldn't see the vet. We were advised to call at nine when the night shift is on duty.

This was the night of the full moon, auspicious for performing rituals. I had already planned, as part of my ritual, to help Taji to pass on to the other side with quickness, ease, and no suffering. I felt that it would be auspicious for Taji to leave his cat body on the night of the full moon. The gods had other ideas.

I did not realize that the power had gone off three times during my *sadhana*, as I was working by candlelight. When I came out of the small temple on the roof, I saw that a light bulb in the laundry area was glowing blue.

At nine we called the veterinary hospital, but no one answered. We finally drove there. A vet came out of the dark building and told us that the power was out. He said that he would call us when it came back on. He never called.

I spent the night on deathwatch. It was a cold night, and Taji was lying in his cat bed in front of a heater. He tried to get up various times, but was weak and wobbly. I lie on the bed fully dressed, staring at the ceiling, and watching the two girl cats for any signs of change. At one point, they both jumped off the bed and circled Taji's cat bed.

That was one of several times that I thought he had passed. My hearing is impeccable, but the cats are even more sensitive, so I relied on them.

At one point, I found Taji standing/crouching at the foot of the bed. He was stiff and cold. My wife woke up and looked at me. I raised my hand and put my thumb and index finger about a centimeter apart to indicate that only a little time was left.

I passed the night like this, filled with a strange energy. Death's presence was palpable. But why did She not just come? I became angry at points. I wanted it all to be over.

Exhausted, I passed out at points. Then I would wake and wonder if the time had come. I spent long moments standing over Taji, watching to see if his ribs were rising and falling. He had become so skinny. His breathing was shallow and irregular. I placed some sacred ash on his head, and told him that it was ok to move on.

Around 5:30, my wife awakened me, saying that Taji was in the bathroom crying. I had not heard. Whenever we found him somewhere else, which usually was not far, we put him back in his cat bed in front of the heater.

A bit after six, I got up and went to the temple to do my morning *sadhana*. When I emerged, the sun was coming up and I could still see the full moon in the western sky. I went to my office and called the veterinary hospital; again, no answer. Again, I felt angry. It seemed that Taji leaving his cat body on the night of the full moon was not to be.

I drifted off again and woke up around nine. My wife called the veterinary hospital. They finally answered and said to bring him. We covered him up and took the whole cat bed. Since we had to wait, and since inside the veterinary hospital was loud and chaotic, I kept Taji outside in the sunlight. In the sunlight, his fur shined, as always, like an angel. There were workmen hanging around nearby, laughing coarsely and joking vulgarly. I told Taji that he would soon be beyond

114

the cheapness of this world. He began to cry. I had never heard him makes such sounds. My wife came to tell me that the vet was ready. Carrying Taji in his cat bed, he cried and stretched out his arms. Then my wife began to cry.

We went into an exam room where the vet and an assistant tried to find a vein in Taji's arm. They had already been shaved when he was in the hospital a couple of weeks previous. I held Taji's head, and he did not complain as they stuck him with a needle a couple of times. They could not seem to get a vein. The vet searched for a pulse with his stethoscope. He could not find one. Taji's head was limp in my hand.

The vet left the room, and I held Taji's head. I felt small movements inside his body. One of his paws and his ear twitched. I was unsure if the moment had come, after watching attentively all night. My wife stroked his fur and cried. When the vet returned, I somehow felt that this was it. Life did not seem to pass into death like an on-off switch; it was much more subtle.

We made arrangements for his cremation. We returned home. I threw away all his food in the refrigerator. My wife picked up the big female cat, Changa, and she made sniffling and sneezing sounds like Taji. I commented that she had never made those sounds before; those were Taji's sounds. My wife said, "Maybe he's saying hi."

The girl cats were playful, loving, and energetic. I thought, "This is life." The vulgar men laughed, and I thought, "This is life."

Monday, 8 December 2014:

I haven't wanted to over-indulge in crying or to entertain thoughts of missing Taji. I want my thoughts to be along the lines of 'he has moved on' rather than that I miss him. I don't want my selfish attachment to hold him here.

I had a dream about him last night. It was a typical scene that he and I played out many times. I am standing at the kitchen counter, preparing food, when I hear a little sniffle behind me. I turn and Taji is standing just behind the corner of the wall leading into the kitchen. He rhythmically shifts his weight from one paw to the other, as if waiting for permission to enter.

Tuesday, 9 December 2014:

I have been eating such crap lately, a lot of meat, cheese, and bread. Today, I made a very spicy green mung bean curry. That and some plain, unsweetened yogurt helped me to get my bowels back in order. I guess I have been indulging because of my sadness.

My family had many dogs and cats when I was growing up. I moved from state to state, from town to town, from parent to parent, so that I learned to not get too attached early in life. Taji taught me a lot, though, about surrender. He displayed an unending devotion to my wife; at times he was in anguish if he could not see her face when she covers it with a pillow in bed. I, in turn, fell for him. I felt that Sri Ganesha was visiting and guiding me through Taji. At some point, I decided that I would serve this cat in any way that he requested.

We picked up his ashes tonight. They came in elaborate packaging. They were sealed in a tiny royal blue nylon bag with handles and a glittery name tag. Inside was a silver box sealed with acrylic gel, inside of which was a thick, black plastic bag with the actual ashes. I ripped open the nylon bag; it looked so ridiculous to me, like athletic wear. Taji was an understated, non-athletic cat. The point of cremating his body was to free him, not to encase him in layer after layer of crap. The ashes were crunchy, like cinders. Looking closely, I could detect little bone fragments.

This was all new to me, and somehow lacked the solemnity that I felt it deserved. When I was a kid, we buried our dead pets in the backyard or in nearby woods. We live in a gigantic city, and we have no yard. Cremation seemed the best option. In the future, I will do this myself. This is not the sort of work that I want to farm out to others. My plan has been to replant six poinsettias (*noche buenas*) (as they bloom at this time of year) in a large pot, and mix the ashes into the soil.

I have been feeling weak, tired, despondent, and it does not help that it has been so cold and gray out. I feel like I want to sleep all day, cuddling up with the remaining girl cats for warmth.

I have also felt somewhat angry with the gods, Santa Muerte in particular. I feel that she has been rather absent or distracted. I could be wrong, but this is my current feeling. I thought, hoped, that Taji would pass on Saturday, the night of the full moon. Saturday is Saturn's day. The full moon, to me, means Shiva as he is a passive ascetic sitting in meditation. Taji died on Sunday morning. Sunday is the sun's day. The sun, for me, relates to the goddess, to Devi/Shakti, because she is active. Maybe it is that my prayers to Kali were heard or heeded over my prayers to Ganesha, Shiva, or Santa Muerte. When I prayed and performed the rituals, I felt that Kali was attentive. I will need to contemplate this more fully.

I've never been an animal rights activist, but I have begun to lean that way. Eating meat and cheese, though I much enjoy their flavors, makes me feel ill physically.

There is a fine line between not entertaining random thoughts that arise unbidden and repression, and it is not always easy to know on which side of that line you're on. Everything here is a gradual unfolding, and it's more likely than not that you will not understand everything immediately. Or, if you feel that you've understood something, that understanding came too soon, and is incorrect. But that's what we try for, with our limited human capacities.

117

Sunday, 14 December 2014:

I've felt so sad, tired, and weak. Today is the first day in a while that I have had any energy or enthusiasm. I keep thinking that I will have a revelation, some sort of epiphany, but the wheels of meaning-making have been grinding slowly.

Friday, 19 December 2014:

I have been really tired, irritable, and angry. I guess part of this is the grief over losing Taji. I really miss him. We adopted a young tiger-striped cat who had been in the cubical next to Taji in the hospital. When Taji didn't want to eat the meat that I brought for him, I would feed it to Zurg (Since we adopt cats, we never get to choose their names.), who would gladly eat it. He is very curious and playful. He seems to never tire of playing and exploring his new home. I can imagine that being cooped up for so long would make one like that.

I've been thinking a lot about the syncretism between Catholicism and traditional indigenous practices in Mexico. One sees many examples of this in small villages. I think that Santa Muerte is a more urban, more popular, and more public example of this syncretism.

Monday, 22 December 2014:

This time of year could not be matched better with the topic of this research. I wander around the streets. The sky is white from the air pollution. The leaves fall from the trees, and dead leaves crunch beneath my feet on the sidewalks. The sound of traffic is never-ending and helicopters hover overhead like giant wasps, shaking the buildings and trees. Everything is dark and gray. While the temperature is not that low, it feels cold for Mexico, and everyone is bundled up. The overall look and feel of the city is what I imagine an industrial revolution steel town to look like, though at the same time futuristic like *Blade Runner*.

I miss Taji greatly. My mood is crappy. I have little motivation or enthusiasm for anything. I always feel tired, and I just want to curl up in bed with the cats.

Monday, 29 December 2014:

I realize that it does not matter much whether Santa Muerte is Mictlantecuhtli or the European Grim Reaper; She is death, and death is universal. As death is part of life, relegating her to a shadow position is unhealthy at best. It is much easier and healthier to integrate shadow elements than to attempt to shun them. My psychotherapeutic practice, as well as simply living life, has shown me that whatever shadow elements we try to disown are instead projected outward onto the world.

Friday, 2 January 2015:

I feel in a weird state. Taji left his cat body ten days ago today. It seems like an eternity.

Sunday, 4 January 2015:

In other types of research approaches, talking about getting stuck and other pitfalls along the way might seem unusual. But this is autoethnography, and every facet of my life is included and important to the overall process and product of the research.

Monday, 5 January 2015:

Today most people went back to work after the winter holidays. I return to the clinic tomorrow after a break of three weeks. It's quite cold and gray. I cleaned out about ¾ of the compost in the roof garden and spread it on the top soil of many of the plants.

Since death has been so present to mind lately, I considered the benefits of this decay we collect in a large plastic box on the roof. Whatever vegetable matter we need to dispose of goes into this compost box. The decomposition of the vegetable matter will provide warmth to the plants, as well as nutrients. It is also food for earthworms and other friendly insects.

I soon put aside the little shovel I was using, realizing that it was easier and faster to use my hands. Digging through the moist black soil, full of earthworms, felt strangely good. My wife passed by, and I suggested that she might like to help me. She shuddered seeing the piles of entangled worms and went back downstairs.

Earth and soil is dead and decaying matter that was once alive. Even the dust in the air that we breathe is made up largely of dead skin. Death is everywhere, and it provides fuel for emerging life.

Many seeds from the foods we consume end up in the compost and, subsequently, in the pots in the garden when I spread the compost as fertilizer. Because of this, many plants have sprouted that we had not intended. Tomatoes are the most abundant, but there are also bell peppers, various chiles, and even cantaloupes.

The garden is always in flux. Things are born, live for a while, wither, and die. Sometimes they return, and other times not. When I first started gardening, I would become frustrated by this impermanence; now I understand that this is how things are, the way of life. So, when unexpected things begin to sprout and grow, including eucalyptus that must be spread on the wind, I am always curious and excited to see what will come.

It has just come to my thought that oil comes from death and decay just the same as everything else. This is not something that I usually think about, as I gave up owning a car twenty years ago. But the pollution caused by emissions from oil/gas burning vehicles is a great problem in this city, as it is everywhere else. Huge deposits of dinosaurs and humans long dead are the contents of petroleum. How sick and sad is our society!

It is strange to me that during this project and all the death attached to it, Santa Muerte herself has seemed to recede into the distance. I am unsure how to describe this. Oftentimes spiritual or mystical happenings are not easily grasped by words, and if they are the effects are diminished.

I am not one of the many anthropologists who travel to Mexico each summer to do their work, their investigations (*research* in Spanish is *investigación*), while they are on paid vacations. I live here wholly, and have done so for eight years. Researching these devotees, these people, I am investigating myself, as we and our fates are more or less one and the same.

Wednesday, 7 January 2015:

We are born alone, live alone, and die alone. Any feeling to the contrary is just a polite illusion. Some people go on about "compassion." That is a given, to suffer together; we are all in pain of existing here. Big deal. Others would say that we should never help another unless asked, because in helping another we are projecting our need onto them. As well, we are saying that we think that they cannot do without our help. In helping them, we are retarding their growth. We actively work so that they will always need our help and will never be able to help themselves. That is quite an insult to another.

121

Thursday, 8 January 2015:

I have had no responses to my recruitment flyers. Tuesday, I decided that enough was enough and I needed to take action. After my job at the clinic, I went to Mercado Sonora, the big witchcraft market. I went from stall to stall, asking, "Are you a Santa Muerte devotee?" Many people said that they were not, even though they were selling Santa Muerte paraphernalia. One woman said that she was a devotee, but would not agree to an interview. I showed her my tattoo and told her that I am a friend of and had interviewed Doña Queta. She replied, strangely, "I cannot give out that kind of information."

Disappointed and frustrated, but undaunted, I moved on. After talking to a few people, I met a chubby lady in her thirties who agreed to the interview. She chose the pseudonym Blanca Rosas (White Roses), which could easily be a normal Mexican name; though I could see in her eyes that she thought it up on the spot. We sat in her tiny cubicle of a stall, in semi-darkness. The interview went well. Striking was a dream she had had where the streets were made of bones.

When asked what religion she is, she said that she is a believer (*creyente*). "I am a 'believer.' I respect all the saints, Santería, Christianity, etc. I have respect for all…the Virgin. I'm not a Catholic; I'm a believer." Like many Santa Muerte devotees, she stresses openness and lack of rigidity in belief.

She said that she believed that Santa Muerte sent me to get her testimony, that it was important that she talk with me. When asked how she came to know Santa Muerte, she replied that she didn't go looking, that Santa Muerte found her.

I left feeling better about the project, even though the interview lacked depth. I planned to return today, but this morning I saw a news item saying that many protests and roadblocks against the government of president Peña Nieto were planned, and the location of Mercado Sonora would be hectic at best.

When I went to the Oxxo convenience store to pay the electric bill, I saw Laura who I had not seen in a few months. I had been told that she no longer worked there. She and I had talked before and we had seen each other at the Tepito shrine. I had been surprised that she hadn't contacted me. She agreed to do an interview, and we set a time to meet in front of another Oxxo on Monday. At least we have each other's numbers now. I am optimistic.

Monday, 12 January 2015:

My wife and I were talking yesterday about an old friend of mine and his parents who were devout Catholics. I had said that I know the Bible and associated things much better than these 'devout' Catholics. This caused fights with my friend in the past. My wife reminded me that Catholics do not read the Bible like Protestants. I grew up in Tennessee and Texas, around many Protestant Christians who could quote many verses of the Bible (the King James version, of course). I remembered this today when interviewing the 19 year old Laura, a goth Santa Muerte devotee. Catholics are used to following a prescribed ritual, while Protestants are more apt to make it up as they go along. This explains a lot about the rote answers that I get in interviews with Catholic Santa Muerte devotees.

I think back to another dead punk friend, Chad Percy from Fort Worth, Texas. He used to ride the rails like a hobo of old, exploring America and experiencing. He would come back with stories about finding the best burrito every in some tiny town in Texas. He was one of the few who *lived* life. Once, when he was approached by some evangelical missionary types wanting to convert him, he said, "Look man, I don't buy retail, I don't buy wholesale, I go straight to the maker," and pointed upwards, smiling his big, silly, toothy grin.

That shut the missionaries up immediately. I'm laughing really hard remembering this.

Wednesday, 28 January 2015:

Today in a taxi to the clinic and recently in the plaza of Tehuacán, Puebla, I had theological discussions with Catholics. I find these talks frustrating and boring. I tend to know the Bible better than these people, and I have thought about it more critically than they have. Christianity is truly a belief system for the weak. It is a way to control people who would probably otherwise run amok. So, I guess there is a need for it. It is still annoying when these people try to convert me to their way of seeing the world (i.e., as a dead rock to be exploited for its resources). I tell them that I am an apostate, that I know everything that they will say, etc., so to just save their breath. I was baptized, not at birth, but by my own choice when I was a kid.

Tuesday, 3 February 2015:

Everything exists because of its concurrent nonexistence. I enjoy the cat sleeping in my lap because there exists the cat not sleeping in my lap. There is day because there is night, love because there is hate, and so on with everything. This is not only a linguistic concept; this is our lives inasmuch as we and our worlds are formed by language.

I had a vision or a dream last night where everything and nothing appeared and reappeared on and off immediately like zeros and ones in a binary system. Our attention does not usually permit us to see a thing in both positive and negative aspects at once, but both aspects are always inherently there and inextricably connected. We tend to focus on what we consider the positive aspects, as if one could exist without its other. We focus on love, and try to push away, ignore, or despise hate. We focus on life, forgetting that we are constantly dying and are being reborn.

I was cooking, chanting mantras aloud, and feeling like my life could be no better. The scent of the cooking food wafted up and all around, and I gave thanks for the food, and for the aromas. I was rhythmically chopping the peppers, chiles, and onions. This is when the earthquake hit. I have not relaxed since. Sometimes I have forgotten, but the effects are still there with me. It goes something like this: "Whatever you love is going to be taken from you. The things that you enjoy, take pleasure in, and embrace, will be ripped screaming from your grasp. And there is not one damn thing that you can do to change that."

So, what option do I have? I started to hate everything. If I hate it, it won't matter if it is taken from me or not. What games we play. My joy of cooking became work, toil, something unappreciated. I resumed my stance of watchfulness, vigilance. If I always stand guard, if I always tense all my muscles, nothing bad can happen to me, to us. Like Atlas, I can bear the weight of the world on my shoulders even if it shifts, as it always does.

Friday, 27 February 2015:

The little boy cat that we adopted is calming down a lot. He is now able to accept caresses without attacking. Last night in bed I put him on my chest, and he stretched out and went to sleep peacefully. It was very sweet.

More frequently I keep having moments of seeing and understanding the positive and negative aspects that comingle in everything. I think of the idea of non-attachment, and I can see more clearly now how this works. I can love unconditionally and wholly, letting myself fall completely, knowing that it will end one day. In fact, that things come to an end makes them that much better, more vivid, more alive, because to live means to die. Every experience is felt more sweetly because it does not last forever. Everything is constantly renewed, constantly changing, ever living, and ever dying.

Waking from a long sleep, I quickly forget the dream I had while sleeping. It lingers hazily, vaguely, before fading away completely. I can picture death being like this, one life fading into another forever. There is no pain or sense of loss, only a continual beginning again. These thoughts buoy my spirits, and enliven me. There is always a new adventure over the horizon, and no need to take anything very seriously.

I think back to a patient who told me that, as a child, she invoked the devil. When her mother asked her who she was talking to, she told her that she was talking to the devil. Her mother would smile. My patient's mother said that God and the devil both came from the same place, they just ended up differently; they were both still holy nonetheless. I have seen similar dualism a lot in my work in Barrio Tepito.

The same patient talked of having a child who was left-handed, and the trials she went through to "cure" him. She said that being born left-handed in Mexico meant that the child was evil, *siniestro* (*sinister*, literally left-hand in Latin).

In both of these cases, there is the privileging of one pole over its opposite. The fact is that both sides exist together inextricably.

Sunday, 1 March 2015:

Last night, my father-in-law and I discussed cremated remains. Cremation is more common in Mexico City than in the US, partly because of lack of space. I think this has something to do with the belief of some Protestant Christians that on the Day of Judgment their former bodies will be resurrected. My father-in-law said that he had never looked at his father's ashes. I told him that our cat's ashes came in a sealed container, but that I had opened it. I was curious to see what they looked like. My father-in-law said, "Very fine, like dust, no?" "To the contrary," I said. The ashes were rather course, and they contained many little white bone fragments where the marrow had been burned away. This probably seems like an odd conversation, but not in Mexico.

Monday, 9 March 2015:

This morning, still in bed in a half-waking state of unremembered dream residue, I was thinking of how people refer to a person's old age, sickness, and decline as the process of death when it is really the process of life. Death is only the point when life ceases. For all we know, death could just be this instant of passing from one phase or state into another. Tibetan Buddhists talk of *bardos*, of liminal states between life and death. I think of just this brief state between sleeping and dreaming and fully waking. There is no pain there, only forgetting, crossing the River Lethe in Greek mythology.

Lately, I often feel that the day gets away from me, that it is difficult to keep up with the hectic pace of life in this gigantic city. It feels like only yesterday that we "fell back" into Fall, and now we are soon to "spring ahead" again. Where does the time go? Mexico City, with its high elevation, does not have the four seasons that I was used to in New England. The weather is almost always the same. It is hot and dry during March, April, and May. During June, July, and August it rains every day around five or six. There is a brief cold spell during November, December, and January. The temperature is nearly always between 40 and 80 Fahrenheit. Having a garden, I can plant and reap all year. I have no feeling of a time of death here. Rather, death and life are always intertwined.

Wednesday, 11 March 2015:

I often consider our cats that sleep most of the time. Their dream lives must seem more real to them than the time they spend awake with us.

Saturday, 11 April 2015:

Many people probably know that Mexican newspapers print photos of dead people. Unless one speaks Spanish and understands colloquial expressions, they probably don't know that the newspapers also print humorous captions beneath the photos of dead people. This is another illustration of the Mexican view of death.

Saturday, 25 April 2015:

Death is only the moment in which we exhale and do not inhale again. Death is shrouded in mystery and symbolized by darkness to show the impossibility of knowing what comes next. In a way, every inhalation is life and every exhalation death; in between these two is a pivot point which is neither. This must be why that in-between state is watched for by the yogi who practices *pranayama*, or breathing exercises.

Thursday, 7 May 2015:

Feeling good is necessarily followed by feeling bad. I believe that if I can maintain a constant low-level bad feeling, I can avoid major tragedy. Obviously, if I drop my hyper-vigilance there will be an earthquake. This is nonsense.

Sunday, 24 May 2015:

Metempsychosis: the transmigration of the soul at death into a new body

Xoloitzcunitles at the Mexico City Zoo

The *xoloitzcunitle*, the Mexican hairless dog, is the Aztec psychopomp that guides the deceased though the Mictlan underworld. Is Santa Muerte a psychopomp? In the Jungian sense, Santa Muerte can be a mediator between the conscious and the unconscious. Death is paired with the unconscious, as the unknown and unknowable. Once what was unconscious is made conscious, its position is changed; it is no longer dark, scary, unknown. We are able to act in consciousness. When we bring something to our conscious awareness, we interact with it in a different way; we are less acted upon by it. When we are consciously aware of something, the first thing we notice is the shifting, changing nature of that of which we are aware. Nothing stays put. Like everything else on the phenomenal plane, objects of consciousness arise, abide for a time, and then pass away. By being conscious of death, of the ephemerality of all phenomena, one can more easily accommodate oneself to life's ever-changing nature and to death.

Saturday, 30 May 2015:

"One is devoured by Time, by History, not because one lives in them, but because one thinks them *real* and, in consequence, one forgets or undervalues eternity" (Eliade, 1967).

Saturday, 6 June 2015:

In relaxation exercises lately, I practice completely letting go. These exercises lead quickly to sleep. At points, I have become afraid that if I let go completely I will die. Then I realize that there is no 'I' to die, but a process that continually changes and never ends.

Last night I visualized that I was lying on my back, as I was in bed, but floating down a slow-moving, cool mountain stream. I rammed into rocks and shattered into droplets of water that dispersed and then reentered the stream. I then realized that I was the water rather than just floating in the stream, that the stream was the flow of Being, and that there was no separate 'I' from the stream, even when the water separated momentarily from the general stream.

Sunday, 7 June 2015:

The more I let go, the easier everything seems to be.

Monday, 8 June 2015:

Life is not the attempt to preserve life.

Tuesday, 9 June 2015:

When you accept something fully, exactly as it is, it begins to change.

Sunday, 28 June 2015:

It is ok to be a little scared of death sometimes. An unexpected thing happened to me through this research. Contrary to what I had thought at the outset of this study, I realized that I fear death. The admission of this vulnerability is all too human, and I feel a little ashamed for it. This is not all tying up neatly as I had imagined that it would. I thought that I would be able to say that my closeness to Santa Muerte means that I am less afraid of death, and maybe I am, but am still a little afraid. For some reason, right now, that feels like a failure.

Wednesday, 1 July 2015:

It's not a matter of believing in Santa Muerte any more than believing in the sun or the moon; death is inevitable. It's just the attitude toward death that is important. It will all be over soon enough.

Monday, 6 July 2015:

I began this study thinking that I do not fear death. Now, I think that I was just not thinking that much about death. I may be terrified of death, but just pushing the thought away.

At least ten of my loved ones have died during my life. These deaths are different, qualitatively, than, say, seeing a dead man on the street in Barrio Tepito or facing the seemingly endless parade of corpses and severed heads in the Mexican newspapers. I think that the latter deaths have a desensitizing effect. These latter deaths are abject and other. I have the feeling that the former deaths are unique and special, while the latter are common and everyday. Probably most people feel this way comparing the deaths of loved ones to those of strangers.

Wednesday, 8 July 2015:

Thinking so much about death has brought up a lot of weepy, melancholy feelings for me. I feel that I am clinging to life more than I ever have. I think a lot about how I love my life and the people who inhabit it. Of course I realize that this sweetness is moreso because it is not endless and tedious. The loss of my self is nothing compared to losing someone that I love. In losing my own life, there is no reflection and nothing to be sad about. I even have more or less irrational fears that when my wife leaves the house, she may not return. But all of this adds to the beauty of life; enjoying time spent with a loved one when we are with them, and missing them when they are gone.

I keep thinking of the last year of my cat's life, when I had to feed him ground beef by hand every day. I became annoyed often that he wouldn't just eat the food from the bowl. Then I would think, "What better do I have to do than this?" It is moments like that that I remember most fondly.

Thursday, 16 July 2015:

I approached, somewhat casually, the *doctora de tanatología* who volunteers at the clinic where I also work as a volunteer in Tepito. Doctor of Thanatology is not a term I've really heard in English, though it is rather common in Mexico. At the clinic, she runs a therapy group for grieving people. As one who studies death and works in Tepito, I thought she might have an interesting take on the cult of Santa Muerte. I asked her if she knew of Santa Muerte. She said, smiling, "Yes! It's satanic!" I was a bit taken aback, but I've become used to the prejudices of my Mexican colleagues. I said, "Surely you must have come across devotees while working here." She said that she had, but that it was her job, as a scientist, to lead people away from superstition. "Don't you think this belief might help someone who has experienced loss, who is grieving?" I asked. "Drugs and alcohol would probably make them feel better, too, but they are not good for you," she shot back. I asked whether she is religious, and she affirmed that she is devout Catholic. "Well, thank you for your time, *doctora*," and I went for a coffee.

This made me think of the customs official at the San Jose, California airport who, upon seeing an image of Santa Muerte in my suitcase, spent an hour searching everything very thoroughly. He asked me, "Are you one of those Santa Muerte people?" And I was wearing a jacket and tie.

Monday, 20 July 2015:

I ran into Laura, the participant of my study, the other day in the Oxxo convenience store where she works. She mentioned that she had not seen me at the shrine in Tepito lately. I told her that I usually go to the shrine on Tuesdays when I am working at the clinic in Tepito. Laura looked confused.

I said that the gatherings on the first of the month are crowded and noisy, that the scene on a Tuesday is much more tranquil; as well, I can talk with Doña Queta and take my time. This, to me, seems better than the situation of feast days where one has to file past the image of Santa Muerte in a long line of devotees. It struck me that Laura likes the crowds. This might be similar to people who only go to church or mass on Sundays or holidays. There is a social element, I suppose, even if, as Laura admits, she doesn't talk to anyone when she is there. I cannot really generalize to say that Mexicans are fond of crowds any more than I could claim that Americans do not like crowds. My personal preference is against crowds and in favor of solitude or the company of a few people. My own spiritual practices, with few exceptions, have always been solitary. My mother, who is a devout Protestant Christian, does not attend church because she sees it as social rather than religious. It's not that the religious and the social cannot combine, but Barrio Tepito is a place that people tend to avoid because of the danger inherent there.

Thursday, 23 July 2015:

For me, the meaning of practicing devotion to Santa Muerte is honoring death, an aspect of life that is usually avoided and neglected, the essence of which is the realization of death in life and life in death. It means recognizing and appreciating the presence of death in the midst of life, in all of my activities. The acknowledgement of the proximity of death makes my life, my experiences, feel richer. I do not mean the gloomy acceptance of death as the end of life, but the acknowledgement that an expiration date means life lived rather than time to be passed or endured.

Wednesday, 5 August 2015:

I had spoken with Laura a few times, as she worked at my local Oxxo convenience store. Once, when returning from a Santa Muerte feast, she commented on my Santa Muerte t-shirt. It turned out that she was also a devotee. When I bumped into her in Tepito on November first, we chatted a little and she agreed to an interview.

Confirming the interview at Oxxo, she suggested that we meet on her day off in the closest Metro station.

She arrived dressed in her gothic Sunday best, a black lace dress that permitted a view of her tattooed arms.

Sunday, 16 August 2015:

I wrote to Dhruvanath, my spiritual teacher in the Nath lineage, asking what I am supposed to do with the taviz that he sent. The taviz is a small object impregnated with a bit of his Shakti (power). He said, "It's not rocket science." I felt like he was saying that I'm stupid. This is how interactions with others have gone lately. I realize that this is my own projection of my insecurity. He said that it is up to me to figure out what to do with the taviz. Still, I felt bad. Now, I see that the taviz is so obvious that my question was probably unnecessary.

I did a ritual for the spiritual cleansing of the house last night. Part of this incorporated the taviz. I sat in meditation, staring at the taviz without blinking. The outlines or shadows of everything on the altar glowed silvery. The candle in front of the image of Kali burned blue instead of the normal white. I could feel the power (Shakti) when touching the taviz. It's hard to describe all of this because it is so subtle. It might be that a normal, non-meditating, person would not notice or perceive anything at all. I tied together some sage from my garden that had been on the altar for a while, absorbing the energy there. I lit the bundle and blew it out to let it smoke. I then waved it in all the corners of the house and around doors and windows, so that the smoke wafted into those areas. I chanted mantra as I did this. The smell was quite strong.

Later, while I was lying in bed, I felt the Shakti of the taviz very strongly. I had felt it before, but I was too active to notice the way that I did while lying down. The feeling was almost overwhelming. I felt that I did not know what to do with the power, and I was afraid of it running out of control or that I would do something unwise. It seemed that whatever I wished came true, was realized. Again, this is very difficult to put into words. And I know from experience that putting these things into words tends to diminish their power. With my mind, my imagination, I put the Shakti from the taviz into my Anahata, heart, Chakra for safe keeping. That seemed to calm things down. Since then, I have felt better, more energetic and alive.

Thursday, 20 August 2015:

Since interacting with the taviz that Dhruvanath sent me, things have been really weird. After the above happened last night, I had a weird night where I felt like I did not sleep. All night, I felt like I was in a state sort of like lucid dreaming. I felt that I was somehow interacting with Shakti all night. It was exhausting in a way, but liberating in another. It is difficult to describe what I mean, and I don't want to analyze it too much because I know from experience that over-analyzing can deflate the experience. I am too intellectual, so I will rely more on feeling here than thinking.

At least twice during the night, I woke up to holding my wife's hand. I cannot remember this happening before (and we've been sharing a bed for a long time). I felt that I was transmitting Shakti to her through this embrace. When that thought hit me, I let go of her hand. I don't want to burden her when I am still going through integrating this Shakti. She has only recently begun a spiritual practice.

I still think a lot about the spiritual emergency that I went through in 2011-2012. That was really difficult, and I had no one to turn to for help to sort it out. That's the sort of thing that I would not want to inflict on another without their willingness and understanding of the consequences. My wife has had her own upheavals to deal with.

I "woke" before seven this morning, feeling that I had not slept. I went to the bathroom and came back to find that my wife was not in bed. All was dark. When I initially got up, I thought she was in bed. I looked at the clock and realized that she had already left for work. Maybe I "woke up" when I heard her close the door. I went back to bed with the three cats piled around me very comfortably.

Today, I ate beef to ground myself. I have been feeling pretty high and energetic. I felt like I expended a lot of energy over the night, though I can't really explain that. As I've written here often, since the spiritual emergency I am cautious and take things in a more slow and measured way. I am a householder, and I am not the only one who has to go through it if I lose my mind again. I am happy. I will resume *sadhana* in the morning.

Friday, 21 August 2015:

When I was in college, I had a class about the Middle Ages. There was a section called The Christian Myth of the Middle Ages, wherein it was pointed out that, contrary to popular belief, Europe was only nominally Christian at this time. Most of the beliefs and practices of the peoples of Europe where still very pagan. Spain conquering Mexico in the late Middle Ages did not make for a purely Christian Mexico. Like their European conquerors, Christianity was forced on the Mexicans.

Before the Conquest of the New World, Spain had been under 500 years of Muslim rule. Islam was a late comer to the Abrahamic traditions of the cult of one masculine god. The supposition that I share with many is that mankind originally worshiped the feminine is contradicted by written archeological evidence that seems to not account that writing was a rather late invention, considered profane by big thinkers like Socrates, and so religious or spiritual matters were not written down but transmitted orally. So, historians and archeologists would have us believe that Vedic-Aryan and patriarchal India is the oldest and most traditional form of spirituality in India. They would also have us believe that the oldest form of religion or spirituality is the Abrahamic patriarchal versions, simply because they are the oldest written examples. Call it intuition, felt-sense, or direct knowing, but I know that the earliest forms of religion or spirituality were matriarchal. Much effort and time could be devoted to mapping the negative influences that the Abrahamic religions have wrought on the West and the rest of the world by extension. But, that is outside the scope of this study.

I will say that various peoples the world over are coming to embrace and reclaim their original and native spiritual practices and beliefs. I think that much of this is attributable to the decline of the Catholic Church, as well as the evidence that these beliefs and practices, aside from being outmoded, have been imperialistic and not all too helpful to the peoples that they have conquered.

In every place that Christianity invaded, they kept most of the local spiritual traditions and put a new Catholic gloss over them. Most Europeans and Americans cannot tell you the meaning of the Christmas tree, or what Easter has to do with rabbits and eggs, because they have forgotten.

I visited an old shaman woman in the mountains of northern Oaxaca who performed a ritual with me. Despite being indigenous and a practitioner of native arts, most of her chanted mantras addressed Christian virgins and saints. This was very off-putting for me.

Tuesday, 1 September 2015:

I first encountered Santa Muerte in the form of statues sold in a market stall in Mexico City when I first came here after eulogizing

138

and burying my best friend, Jacky, of 21 years. I was still crushed by the loss, and ephemerality and death were very much on my mind. It was appropriate that I should meet Santa Muerte at this time. I recognized her as Death, as the Grim Reaper. It was my old friend, Mexican guide, and now wife who explained to me that this was a local folk saint, and not the European Grim Reaper, although the image is more or less the same. When I laid eyes on her, I felt her in my heart. I had to know more about her. I purchased a statue then. That was in March 2007.

Since then, I have been a devotee of Santa Muerte. Part of the reason that I wanted to do this study was to compare my views and practices of devotion with those of other devotees in Mexico City. Less than a year after I first encountered Santa Muerte, I was living in Mexico City and practicing psychotherapy as a volunteer at a community mental health clinic in Barrio Tepito, Santa Muerte's home.

Thursday, 3 September 2015:

My spiritual orientation and practice is as a Shaiva-Shakta Tantrika, meaning that I am a devotee of Shiva and Shakti, the Hindu Deva and Devi (often translated as god and goddess). I am a pagan, a polytheist, and pantheist. I believe in and venerate a number of deities and I believe that everything in the phenomenal world is a manifestation of God, or the infinite and eternal play (*Lila*) of Shiva's Shakti. Given this, it is easy for me to recognize Santa Muerte as a manifestation of the goddess or Shakti.

I am not a Christian or a Catholic, though I was once. Because of the differing Christian sects of my parents, I attended both Lutheran and Catholic schools. I was a pretty pious believer in God, and I even got baptized of my own volition at age 8. I became more interested in finding a transcendent element that I felt Christianity lacked.

Thursday, 24 September 2015:

I ran into Laura at the Oxxo today. She asked about the Rosario de Santa Muerte next week on Thursday, the first of October. She asked if it was ok to go in the morning rather than in the afternoon when most people go. I said that it's permissible to visit the shrine anytime you want. She mentioned that more people would be there in the afternoon. I said that I go on Tuesdays when I am at the clinic nearby, that visiting the shrine when there are fewer people around means that you get more quiet time with Her, with Santa Muerte.

She seemed to feel guilty about having to go in the morning because of a work schedule conflict. I told her that the rosaries used to be at midnight in the past. Now, it is a rare few that are there at midnight. "Barrio Tepito changes at 5 or 6 at night. The people on the street change, and what is being sold changes. People who live there will tell you that it's a good idea to be out of there by five or six, and certainly before it gets dark." Laura said, "But She is Death! She controls all of this!" "I know," I said. "If you are there at night, nothing bad is going to happen to you. We all know that. We are all brothers and sisters there."

Saturday, 26 September 2015:

One life versus many lives. How does the belief in one unique life inform the psychology of death? None of the participants I have spoken with believe that we live just one life. It seems that we all believe in a form of reincarnation.

Some notes I wrote down in Bogotá, Colombia:

Practice of devotion to Santa Muerte is tantric, or it can be. I will not here go into an exhaustive description of Tantra. What is important to know is that Tantra means doing, practice over theory, combined with total acceptance. Through tantric practice, a psychological change occurs that changes the way the practitioner experiences the world. Tantra is not religious; it is amoral. (Osho, 1972) It is not intellectual or philosophical.

Santa Muerte could be one of the *Mahavidyas*, the feminine tantric wisdom deities.

"All fear is basically death-oriented" (Osho, 1972).

The "funny" thing with our modern "science" is that one can claim anything and provide enough evidence to make it so.

In Mexican folk religious practices, there is *Brujeria*, witchcraft or black magic, and *Santería*, white magic. Distinctions such as *magia negra* or *magia blanca* may be applied, but no one moving in this world denies the existence or the efficacy of magic. Most Westerners would call magic unscientific or pseudo-science, the latter typically is applied to things that are very much scientific but currently out of vogue because of politics. There is little difference between science and magic, though the proofs of the latter are often difficult to qualify or quantify. Magical effects are often subjective, and there is difficulty in establishing a causal chain. There are psychological effects that work this way, such as placebo and nocebo, that one's belief in the efficacy affects the efficacy. These things seem weird and foreign to Westerners and Christians, but they are very much a part of indigenous life and spirituality the world over.

Wednesday, 30 September 2015:

The mind plays tricks. I notice that I can observe my mind working, as though I am standing behind it. So, I am not my mind. Descartes was not enlightened. My mind has an interest in its own survival. Meditation specifically is a danger to the mind's survival. The mind will make excuses, and create ways to block meditation from happening. The mind can only operate in the past or in the future. In the present moment, which is all that *really* exists, the mind cannot live.

When everything is calm and perfect, the mind looks for problems, for difficulties. The mind is not needed if everything is perfect; the mind has to solve problems. The mind gets scared if it is idle and unneeded. It has to be active; it has to do something. That is the illusion that it has built. When no problem exists, the mind creates problems to be solved, just to keep alive and active.

Tuesday, 13 October 2015:

There are Mexican newspapers like *El Grafico*, *La Prensa*, *Metro*, and others that print color photographs of dead people. These are people killed in whatever manner, and the photos are graphic. Often the images are of car crashes. Just as often, the images portray the violence of the drug war: naked and burned bodies hanging from highway overpasses, a line of numerous severed heads, naked bodies bound with duct tape with heads and genitals removed, naked dead bodies of men arranged in homosexual positions, and usually accompanied by *narco mensajes* (messages from whichever cartel to another cartel or the police or military or the government warning that this is what happens to people who cross them). There is even a cheaply printed magazine called *Alarma* that is devoted solely to this type of reportage known in Mexico as *nota roja* (red note, the red signifying blood). *El Grafico* calls this section of the paper simply *la roja*, the red.

When I first encountered such publications, I was taken aback. The United States press is often prevented by the government from publishing even images of flag-draped coffins of soldiers. These images are often difficult to avoid, as they are displayed at news kiosks on every street corner.

Over time, I have become somewhat desensitized to these grizzly images. I assume that most Mexicans have been affected similarly. It is often said that, in Mexico, life is cheap. But I think that there is another way of looking at this. In the West, life is so precious as to not admit the presence of death, that it goes hand-in-hand with life.

Friday, 23 October 2015:

Since I moved to Mexico in the beginning of 2008, the drug war of Presidente Calderón and now Peña-Nieto has claimed over a million lives.

I just watched an American made documentary called *Narco Cultura*, and I was aghast. There are Mexican-Americans in Los Angeles who make *narco corrido* music and movies without ever having been to Mexico. They, like the Hollywood gangster rap that came before, are capitalizing on a glorified version of an ultra-violent Mexico of myth.

I am very troubled by this. These LA "Mexicans" or "Chicanos," are Mexican in the same way that the characters in the TV show *The Sopranos* are Italian. They glorify an isolated aspect of a culture that they really do not know. In the documentary, the singer of a band from Los Angeles goes to a Santa Muerte temple to get a blessing for his safety when he visits Mexico for the first time. He admits that he is scared, but this does not stop him from his arrogant and idiotic posing.

143

Tuesday, 3 November 2015:

We didn't set up an *ofrenda* for Day of the Dead this year. I did not attend the Santa Muerte feast day this year. We have been in the process of moving to another house, and it has consumed quite a lot of time and energy. The absence of these holidays is hardly noticed. For me it brings into clear relief that these things are kinda silly. We condense things that are important, omnipresent even, into one day of acknowledgment and assume that this will suffice for the year. This, to me, is all too much like the Sunday churchgoer who half-heartedly gives a piece of one day to God, and then resumes his quotidian ignorance. This is not the pantheism that is reality. Come to think of it, this practice of sectioning off a bit of life is rather insulting. If God is all, is in everything, *is* everything, then why the cutting up and compartmentalizing of the experience of God?

While I am intellectually inclined, I have always noted the gap between theory and practice. When I encounter a theory, I have to test it out in real life. Unless I can put it into practice, it is useless to me. Knowledge *obtained* through books is not the same as knowledge *attained* through experience.

While growing up, I too often saw the pious observances of Christians who went to church very seriously and reverently, and maybe even felt or experienced something of God, but left all of that behind in the room in which it took place to resume their normal, Godless lives. How could I not be left cold by such "religious" practice? By extension, it is likely that I see a connection between institutional religious observance and communal religious practice.

I have my whole life seen a privileging of quantity over quality. I see an extension of this in the mass religious festival where validity seems to come from quantity. A religious festival gains attention by the number of attendees, while the lone practitioner passes without notice, even though his experience of God is likely to be deeper than that of those attending the mass.

Thursday, 19 November 2015:

Regarding my Santa Muerte research, I feel that much of the interest from outsiders revolves around the so-called *occult*. *Occult* means *hidden*, but oftentimes this simply means that what is hidden is hidden from people who are not actively seeking. Another word, *sinister*, comes to mind. *Sinister* means *left-hand*. In traditional cultures, the dirty work is done with the left hand. The most common example of this is cleaning after defecating; this is a task for the left hand. A Muslim will not touch the Koran with the left hand. There are other spiritual traditions, namely Tantra, that are known as left-hand. I am a practitioner of Tantra, and for me everything is God so nothing is unclean or off-limits. However, all too often, *occult* or *sinister* is taken to mean *evil*. Evil is a dualistic concept like the others. As far as moral wrong-doing, I see none of that in the cult of Santa Muerte.

Monday, 30 November 2015:

Our little boy cat, Zurg, got out of the compound somehow. That was heart wrenching, as there was little we could do. I fell asleep repeating mantra in my head, so that I was conscious of continuing the repetition while I slept. My wife was crying. I kept saying, "He's strong and smart. He'll be back," though I had my doubts. It was weird how he seemed to just disappear with no trace.

I felt that I had to remain strong for my wife and to influence the desired outcome. At 4:30 in the morning, he was clawing at the gate. He was covered in motor oil and very tired. He's been so sleepy since he came back, perhaps traumatized. We'll never know what adventures he had.

145

My wife has been hysterical a lot lately, saying that she is a loser. She gets into spirals of comparing herself to others that are not profitable and just annoying. There is really never any point in comparing ourselves to others; this is just a trick of the mind. I feel that the more I live in isolation from others, the world, the happier I am. These comparisons are meaningless in the absence of the other. Probably there is still an internalized other, but that other can be constructed in a more positive way. Anyhow, I constantly feel led to thoughts that I don't want to think, and I feel like I need to help my wife to be aware of the tricks of the mind. This becomes exhausting, and I want some respite.

The Spanish language is incredibly poor. There are far fewer words in Spanish than in English. But the idiocy and inadequacy does not stop there. When my wife's armoire was eaten by termites, people kept saying that it was eaten by moths. Moths don't eat wood, they eat wool! I have lost many sweaters to moths, none to termites. When my niece-in-law had a red spot on her cheek, her father said she was bitten by a fly. There are few biting flies in the world, probably none here in Mexico. She was bitten by a mosquito, technically in Mexican, a little fly. Because of the poor Spanish language, Mexicans are much more emotional and expressive. It's like when I was a kid, my parents told me that unintelligent people use profanity because they lack the vocabulary to better express themselves. Mexicans actually have these words to express these things, but do not use them, or use them wrongly. I very well understand that a word is not the thing it represents, but we strive to get as close as possible to the truth even if it falls short. Are Mexicans just lazy? No one seems to care. Whether or not the words exist to express what needs to be said, Mexicans seem to not care which words are chosen. The truth, The Real, can never be expressed in language. Does that mean that we simply abandon language? This is hard to take for me who has always strived to get as close to the truth as possible in writing.

The weakness of the Spanish language is something that is a bit contentious between me and my wife, even though she speaks five languages fluently. She feels that I am disparaging of Mexican culture when I point out the lack in the Spanish language. Tonight, I said, "Either we choose to be one with nature and live in loin cloths or we use the most precise tool given us for the task of communication." This, of course, angered her.

Wednesday, 2 December 2015:

Throughout this research project I have tried to come to terms with death. I started out thinking, believing, that I did not fear death. I have long contemplated death, and I now realize that I fear death more than I did before engaging in this project. As humans, we are born with the imperative to die, and fear of death is probably one of the most human of traits. Not to sound cliché, but I better realize now the importance of living in the present moment. The past and future are not living but activities of the mind. Have I become better at living, at being in the moment? I have gotten better at it. I think that I am more aware than when I started this project. I am not sure that this is a goal to be reached as much as a process to be accepted and even embraced; this is life.

Thursday, 3 December 2015:

I've looked for the dark side of Santa Muerte, if one exists. This dark side is what seems to attract or repel people equally. She is formidable; you can't look, but you can't look away. She is death. She is dark, as opposed to the light of life. These are things that are built into the idea of death, into Santa Muerte. These are the things of horror films that equally attract and repel, depending on the person.

147

Death is not something that anyone escapes; it is only one's attitude toward death that means anything.

That said, I have met some people who view the cult in darker ways than the already marginal mainstream of the cult. There are exceptions. But I prefer to view this as psychodrama, which is often part of magic.

I report on this aspect with some trepidation, because I am a devotee of Santa Muerte and want to present her in the most positive light. So, I admit my bias. While I do not see this aspect as negative, I know that I might be in the minority. I've been in and around this community since 2007, and I think that so much exposure has desensitized me to many or the more sensational aspects of the Santa Muerte cult.

Friday, 11 December 2015:

Most of the people who read this will not be those living in Latin America and will likely not understand that Catholic festivals take place every day of the year in one place or another. These festivals are charming for foreigners, less so for the people living here. Picture days and nights of people screaming, of explosions of fireworks without color that sound like gunshots, of bells ringing. No one can reasonably be expected to sleep, or even watch TV without the volume turned up all the way. There is no escape. And what about the people who have to work the next day? Western companies based in Mexico pay bonuses to employees who simply arrive to work on time. In the US, that bonus is that one gets to not be fired.

Wednesday, 16 December 2015:

Today I interviewed another participant for the study. He wanted to be called Johnny (Mexicans write this as Jhony.) He is a *sicario*, a hit man, an assassin for one of the cartels. His has been the most interesting interview thus far. I wonder now if I should try for more interviews, reaching out to others that might be as interesting. He was also the first to contact me via my website. He was also the one most concerned with anonymity. I had not considered stressing anonymity, as this is typically not important to Mexicans. Out of 712 hits on my website, he is the only one who has actually contacted me through the website.

In all of the interviews I've done, without exception, everyone has agreed that the colors of candles or images of Santa Muerte are of purely commercial significance. Everyone says, "If you believe that a particular color has this effect, then it does." This is placebo, which is a real thing. As a psychologist and a devotee-practitioner, this lines up with my own thoughts. If it is the mind that produces these images and thoughts, then why is a dream less real than a waking event?

Johnny did not talk much about his profession, and I did not press him. He said that he is a devotee because death is all around him. He is a death dealer. He kills who he is told to kill. He said that quick and simple is his preferred method. He does not torture people; there are others who do that. He only uses a gun, never a machete or some other barbaric means of dispatching the target. He does not seem to take pride in his work, and that he is doing just what he was taught to do from an early age.

He said the same thing that we all say: We all meet Death sooner or later, but some of us will already be on first name terms with Her. He said that we are all already dead, we just don't know it. He added, "If there is a God, where is He? To me there is only La Muerte. If there was a God and God was good, he would stop all of this."

He had a depressive aspect to him. He seemed cold and sad. I think he wanted to confess to someone, maybe to someone more secular. I was glad to be there to receive his confession. Hardly anyone believes in confessing to priests anymore. The Roman Church has lost so much respect.

I assured him that our interview would always be kept in the strictest privacy. I would never reveal him to anyone, no matter what.

He shed a few tears. I don't think he particularly enjoys his work, and that can make all the difference in one's life. But, things in this country are complicated. He was born into this life. He has to do what is necessary to survive.

Saturday, 2 January 2016:

I am really tired of the whole Guadalupe-Reyes holiday series. The last one is Wednesday. That is *Reyes Magos* (Magician Kings, the Three Wise Men). We now live in Pueblo de los Reyes. So the Three Wise Men are the patron saints of this neighborhood. I'm really not looking forward to the festivities. There have been too many festivities. They are still setting off fireworks as I type this. It feels like a war. These fireworks (*cohetes*) don't produce pretty colors or forms in the sky, only really loud noise. Kids are out doing this all night, often right in front of the house. The effect is really jarring. There are plenty of drunks in the streets. I try to be in before nightfall. I am trying to be neither for nor against things, and just accept everything as it is. That has been going well. It is not always easy.

Sunday, 10 January 2016:

It's Sunday, the 10th of January, and the fireworks are still going off. There is no more holiday. Oh! There's a marching band in the street! Jesus! Every time an explosion goes off, I am jarred and pulled into the present moment. I am becoming more comfortable, in a way, with these noises. I'm getting a lot from reading Osho. Surrender.

Saying 'no' strengthens the ego; saying 'yes' dissolves the ego. Life feels better when accepting everything just as it is.

Sunday, 17 January 2016:

In religions, generally, there is an *exoteric* and an *esoteric* aspect. The exoteric aspect is the outside, observable, objective form seen in such things as masses, group rituals, and gatherings. The esoteric aspect is experiential, individual, and subjective, taking such forms as meditation, prayer, and solitary ritual. There are many public religious rituals in Mexico. Since these rituals are public and so prolific, it is easy to view and study them. Esoteric forms of religion are more elusive. Yet, it is in the esoteric form that I find meaning.

While I have, at times, enjoyed the Santa Muerte gatherings in Barrio Tepito and in Ecatepec, it is my alone time with Santa Muerte that has had a greater impact on my spirituality and growth as a person. An analogy can be drawn between watching a game and playing a game. Though the levels of participation can vary greatly across participants in exoteric rituals, the rituals remain external and public. The esoteric aspect cannot be spoken of. To each their own. It is subjective and private. Words fail to describe it.

Tuesday, 19 January 2016:

I think of *religion* as exoteric and mundane, and *spirituality* as extraordinary and esoteric. I am more interested in the latter. Exoteric religious practices are about doing prescribed acts, often with the hope of something like an afterlife in an otherworldly heaven. Esoteric practices are about experiencing heaven in the here and now, about the transpersonal and the transcendent. They teach a practitioner how to live in the world without being of the world.

Friday, 22 January 2016:

Often the esoteric is also referred to as the occult. The occult makes one think of secret societies and ancient books of arcane knowledge. But while *occult* means *hidden*, the less glamorous sense in which this should be taken is as *subtle* rather than *obvious*. Occult religious practices often apply the same rigor as so-called scientific experiments, with the results however being subjective and personal rather than objective and general. Knowledge is state specific. It is difficult, if not impossible, to understand state-specific phenomena across states of consciousness (Tart, 1972).

Thursday, 4 February 2016:

Something or someone was always there, and now is not. It is not easy, coming to terms with loss, with the ephemeral nature of everything in the phenomenal world. One need not harden one's heart, steeling oneself in expectation of the inevitable. One cannot withhold affection for fear of disappointment, of loss. By doing so, one does not live fully. If one is in the present moment, that eternity is life. It is only in reflection, in memory, that the sadness seeps in.

A couple of times this week, the boy cat has somehow gotten onto the roof of the house that is connected with the roofs of other houses in this village. Many cats roam here. There are branches and leaves on the roof where neighborhood cats like to hang out.

The first night, I saw the boy cat on the roof, and could see that he couldn't figure out how to get down. I am still unsure how he got to the roof. I got the ladder and climbed up. As I brought the cat down in my arms, he was terrified of falling and clawing me badly. Ignoring the pain, I held him in my arms and comforted him. I thought of times as a child when my mother had to help me down from trees where I had climbed too high.

Last night, he was on the roof again. I watched him walk gracefully along the ledge. He looked at the people and cars passing in the street below, up at the stars in the cobalt sky, and down at the barking dogs in the adjacent yard. These are new sights for him, and I felt like I was seeing them newly through his eyes. "He's adventurous and wants to experience the world," I thought. So, I let him enjoy his play. I felt a gladness tinged with pain in my heart, as would a father watching his son step precariously into a new world without the old familiar supports.

When I tried to fetch him from the roof, he ran from me. I suppose he remembered how scary it was to descend the ladder. So, I didn't pursue him. I let him go free to explore and learn. I know that he will return when he has had his fill of adventure. Still, I could not help worrying a bit. I set aside my worry, realizing that it only serves to upset me. Safety is rather overrated. Safety doesn't provide experience. For experience, in order to truly live, one has to venture out and take risks. This cat is smart and capable. I have to let him go and trust that he will return when he's ready. If you love something, you cannot hold it in your grasp; you have to let it go.

Wednesday, 10 February 2016:

Transpersonal inquiry: Ask Santa Muerte, "What do you want to teach me? What do you want me to learn?" Methods: dream incubation, contemplation.

Reply: If you want to do something, do it. At the same time, don't worry about it. Don't worry about completion, about success or failure, and don't worry about consequences. You can accept responsibility if you like, but this act will only help to strengthen the ego and create karma. What is the difference between doing and not doing?

Friday, 12 February 2016:

Once when in a public transport van going through the endlessly curvy mountain roads of Oaxaca, I noticed that each time we passed a shrine to a saint or a virgin all of the old women passengers made the sign of the cross. I began to adopt this practice myself. There are shrines all over the place, and I notice that by crossing myself when encountering them, I am constantly recognizing the presence of the divine.

This practice has included the Santa Muerte shrines, and has extended to rubbing and kissing the Santa Muerte figure that I keep on my keychain. That part usually takes place when I am leaving the house, as I am locking up, and I have a notion of the protective power that she provides.

To many, Mexicans included, crossing yourself or kissing an image of a spiritual figure smacks of superstition. But this practice is not some compulsive turning a light switch on and off; it is a mindful recognition of the sacred that permeates everything. By bringing to mind the sacred, even for a moment, the world is transformed.

Superstition tends to carry a negative connotation, and is prohibited by the Catholic Church as perversely over-religious. An odd condemnation, indeed. Presumably, the Pope is *just religious enough*. But is crossing oneself before a shrine superstitious, or could it be that the Catholic Church simply means to maintain its control over all ritual?

"Our self to live must go through a continual change and growth of form, which may be termed a continual death and a continual life going on at the same time. It is really courting death when we refuse to accept death; when we wish to give the form of the self some fixed changelessness; when the self feels no impulse which urges it to grow out of itself; when it treats its limits as final and acts accordingly" (Rabindranath Tagore, *Sadhana*, cited in Govinda, 1976).

I wanted to go into the study and practice of Santa Muerte with the fewest preconceptions. I wanted to be empty, so as to be filled. I wanted to feel that I knew nothing so that I might learn something.

Now, the comings and goings of the boy cat are normal for me. They were always normal, as the rising and falling of the abdomen when breathing in and out; but now I notice the arising and passing as normal. Gone and back again!

Doing the dream incubation has not yielded much beyond the first night. I've had no visions of Santa Muerte. Perhaps that is Her way, silence.

Tuesday, 16 February 2016:

After yesterday morning's excitement (I really felt that I went into *Samadhi*, but that is not easy to talk about.), everything went downhill. My friend Antonio cancelled our lunch because he ate some bad chicken and got diarrhea. The boy cat got stuck high up in the tall tree in the garden. My wife was mean and bitchy, yelling at me and being awful. I had to pretty much beg for an apology, and then it was like, "Screw you! I'm sorry!" I tried everything I could think of to try to get the cat down, but he's too high up.

My neck and shoulders ached and I was dizzy from looking up into the tree. I hardly slept. The way my wife treats me constitutes abuse. I fear her and I try to please her. It would be easier and less painful if she beat me physically. I understand that she is irritable and stressed out, but it's not right that she take her anger out on me. I lie in anguish most of the night, hearing the cat's anguished cries and thinking too many thoughts. I kept thinking, "Who is this 'I' that is hurting? This 'I' doesn't really exist."

I have been able to note these actions of consciousness in meditation, but it is harder in normal life. When confronted with someone yelling at you, asking questions to which you must respond, how do you simply notice it and move on? I guess I am still looking for some kind of justice, fairness, and reason. The world and people are often not reasonable. That we be nice to each other, and not be mean to each other seems very reasonable to me.

I know that this is a test put before me. There is something I am meant to learn here. I have made a lot of progress quickly, after what seems like a long time of slogging along in my *sadhana*. It is one thing to have a transpersonal experience in meditation, and another to stabilize that experience and bring it into daily life.

I have to continue on. I had lots of thoughts of not wanting to be with my wife. But it is probably here that I need to be. These difficulties don't arise in isolation, and they are things that I need to bring to my awareness and go through (transcend). If there is unpleasantness, it is because of past karma, and I have to pay up sooner or later.

As I type, I can hear the boy cat crying in the tree. My wife called a tree cutting service, and they are coming in about four hours. That's a long time to wait. I suffer with that cat.

My wife seemed happier, calmer on the phone this morning. She can easily forget her past behavior.

Yesterday's fighting, as always with women, kept circling back and picking up unrelated threads. This makes things so much more confusing and confounding. She seems to think that I do nothing, and that I should be there to do whatever is necessary. I do all of the house things, and I even took over cleaning the litter box. I felt bad for the cats that my wife neglected it, and they started pooping in the garden. That's not good for the plants.

I am fine with cleaning the thing. I do it every day, so that it doesn't become a big task. Maintenance is the key. I guess that is true for everything. It is more important to bring a problem continuously into awareness than to solve it (That's from Jung.). I am fine and happy to do all the housework, but I wish that it was appreciated. Like Jacky's dad used to say, "Wish in one hand, shit in the other, and see which one fills up the fastest."

I should just continue to be aware, to notice the actions of consciousness, and let them go. I shouldn't try to change things or look for a reward or for justice. This is karma, and karma will do its thing.

Later: The cat is down. Our neighbor, Hugo, climbed up and got him with great difficulty. He was very brave. I am happy to have met him. I gave him 500 pesos. It's weird how things work out. The tree cutting people that my wife called were going to charge us 2500 pesos. That is a lot of money, considering. But I would have paid whatever they asked. If I gave that much to Hugo, he would think we are rich and stupid. I wanted to keep a neighborly amicability between us.

I can still hear the cat crying, even though he's now asleep on the sheep skin before the shrine on the floor behind me.

Wednesday, 17 February 2016:

There are so many people who have nervous breakdowns and psychotic breaks. I never felt that I had that luxury. If I were to break, who would take care of things? I always had to be the sober, responsible one. If I broke down, who would have taken care of me? If someone had taken care of me, it would have been proof that I can't take care of myself.

Later: What a difficult day! After the *Samadhi* experience Monday morning, I felt so wonderful. All of that started going downhill after Antonio canceled our lunch date. He did not take well me saying this when we met today. Monday, I had wanted to share with him how great I had been feeling, and I wanted to show him the vipassana meditation technique that has helped me so much. Today, all of that was a shadow. I later realized that I was trying to convey state-specific knowledge to someone who doesn't even believe in such states of consciousness.

Antonio is a really bourgeois conventional person. He's not stupid, he's an intellectual, but he is like most people. He kept saying that I should have kids, buy a house, etc. I told him that I am not a normal person, that I've seen the misery of normal people (I see these things on a daily basis as a shrink.).

"People are really attracted to new chains, of enslaving themselves like all the other stupid slaves, and my wife and I don't want that." Advice like "plan for the future" sounds good in this phenomenal world; it's the epitome of responsibility. But the future is an illusion. If you can't live well right now, what do you think the future will be like? The secular concept of the future is like the Christian concept of Heaven. But the only thing that is real is *this very moment.* We went round and round with him telling me that I am immature, etc., until it culminated in me throwing some money on the table and leaving.

He said that the married-with-children woman he's seeing made an appointment for him to see a shrink. I said, "If it's a Mexican shrink, they'll probably tell you you're an adulterer and you're going to hell." He took this as an offense against his dead mom, who was a shrink. He held his index finger and thumb together and said, "You are this compared to my mom!" As if he would have any idea how his mom was as a shrink, never having been her patient. But I get it. It was all messed up. My thousands of hours of sessions and viewing other peoples' sessions is meaningless here.

No one wants you to change, for you to get better, because that threatens their sense of I-ness. Friends and family are the biggest obstacles to change, to realization of the self, because their very existence is connected with yours. Rare is the person who can truly say to another, "I support and love you and I wish you well in whatever way transformation and transcendence take you; to say to another, when they die, 'Leave this place and don't come back!'"

After that, I went to my in-laws' house. They offered me coffee and we chatted for a long time. We played with the baby and the cats, and it was a nice experience, one that I'm likely to repeat.

Back in Coyoacán, I ran into Hugo (the neighbor who got the boy cat out of the tree) on the street. We talked, and it turns out he is a Santa Muerte devotee. I showed him my tattoos, and he said that he doesn't have a Santa Muerte tattoo, but one of Kali. I was taken aback. I told him that I am also a devotee of Kali, and that I had prayed to her when the cat was stuck in the tree. We were both silent and beaming with smiles at this revelation. I am still a little awe-struck. How nicely things connect!

It's obvious to me that I am meant to learn something from these experiences (especially the negative ones), something that Antonio found ridiculous. I have been trying to observe my typical and automatic reactions to things (stimuli). In this way, I hope to be able to find patterns and to, at least, be aware of them. I mean to watch times and situations in which I get angry, tense, irritable, sad, et al.

I find that I get irritable and sometimes angry when I feel that I "have to do everything." I have been taking on more things to do, such as washing the dishes, all of them, most of the time. Knowing this and agreeing to do this, I feel freed by it. But I know that this is, in a way, hedging my bet. What happens when I am called on to do something extra that I don't expect? That is a better test, probably, of what is really going on that makes me feel angry.

I have a sense of fairness, individualism, and egalitarianism where everyone does their part. That seldom works out in practice. Am I able to do whatever is called of me to do whenever I am called? This is a question to ponder.

Oftentimes, I offer to do things, to take on tasks, in order to help others, and the offer is met with anger and rejection. I can't control anyone else, and we all bump against each other constantly. I really want to make things easier for others and, by extension, myself. I think of this as a form of enlightened interdependence. Maybe I am wrong. I mean, this is why communism sounds good but has never worked. Some people are caring and considerate, while others are not. There is an aesthetic beauty to that, I suppose.

Thursday, 18 February 2016:

I feel off. Meditation was difficult this morning. I keep thinking, turning over stupid shit in my head. When I would note, "doubting," or, "discouraging," I would feel a chill run down my spine and know that Shiva was there with me. Another time when I noted the above, Zerg, the boy cat, came and lied down next to me, nuzzling me. I am not alone. I am taken care of and watched over. I know this. It has been shown many, many times. And still I have doubts. I need to simply note, "Thinking," and move on.

If the *Samadhi* experience of Monday morning was a peak experience, I suppose I am now feeling the resulting trough experience. Maybe I was given a taste of what is possible so as to inspire me to continue the practice. But trying to replicate an experience is always doomed to failure. Thinking really seems to ruin everything. I need to get my mind under control.

Friday, 11 March 2016:

Activos (those who use inhalants, solvents, etc. to get high) live in small tribes on the streets of Mexico City. I have been familiar with a couple of them since working at the clinic. Unlike other people living on the street, the *activos* have never asked me for anything. They have occasionally accepted a cup of coffee, a cigarette, or some food, but they've never asked me for these things. One *activo*, called Fulcio because he resembles a comic strip character of that name, acts as a sort of unofficial doorman at the clinic. He has been there since before I came in 2009. At that time, he was 16 years old.

An American who was in charge of the dormitories above the clinic tried to get Fulcio to stay there, but said that he would have to give up drugs first. In a rare moment of lucidity, Fulcio responded, "Would you give up your wife?" Fulcio wasn't interested.

An *activo* saw that I was taking pictures. He gestured for me to take his picture. A large joint dangled from his mouth. Some of his front teeth were missing. He held his Santa Muerte statue cradled in one arm, his other hand holding his *activo* rag soaked in whatever solvent was to his liking. He was shirtless. His skin was smooth and brown and here and there was a cheap-looking, faded tattoo on his chest. It was not easy to make out what he said, as he was drooling and slurring his speech. I wondered if he would allow me to interview him, whether I could understand well enough if he did, and what were the ethical implications of interviewing someone so obviously under the influence.

But *activos* are a significant presence in Barrio Tepito and in the cult of Santa Muerte. While *activos* appear zombie-like, typically drooling and mumbling, Luis Miguel had the clarity of mind to be at a given place at a given time and to bring his Santa Muerte statue with him. Maybe he was a part-timer, not one of the *activos* who live on the street. However, from where I stood, I couldn't see any difference. He reached out and touched my beard, caressing it. He told me that I'm pretty (*bonito*). I thanked him, blushing.

Monday, 14 March 2016:

To ask the question whether Santa Muerte is a real, embodied personality we would also have to ask whether you or I are real, embodied personalities. This sort of question from scientific unveiling seeks to remove the mystery that is part of the workings of Santa Muerte. Part of Santa Muerte's effect, and indeed that of any religious or spiritual figure, is through mystery that cannot be held or dissected by positivistic science.

Sunday, 17 April 2016:

Today while my wife and I were taking a walk in our neighborhood, a man offered me a joint for a cigarette. I think he was making a joke. I gave him a cigarette and a light. As I walked away, he said that he likes my Santa Muerte. I lifted my t-shirt sleeve to show my tattoos, and he said something about them being cool. He couldn't have seen the tattoos before I raised my sleeve. I assume that Hugo told him about me. This is a small village. I am happy that I am seen as fitting in.

Tuesday, 26 April 2016:

Several patients I've treated at the clinic in Tepito have told me that, as children, they venerated, prayed to, and often asked favors of the devil. Part of this is rebellion, but another part is the nature of syncretic Catholicism. In Catholic conquests, indigenous spiritualties, beliefs, and practices are incorporated into Catholicism. Indigenous deities become saints and virgins under the Catholic banner. At the same time, not all occurrences of indigenous, pagan spiritual practices are suppressed and punished so that they linger on up to the present. Since all Catholics pray to saints and virgins as intercessors to God, then how different is the devil? In the tantric sense, if God is all and everything, then the devil can be seen as another of God's manifestations. And if one cannot ask God for certain things, then the devil might seem like a reasonable alternative.

Wednesday, 4 May 2016:

I am following the flow of the diary to give a linear continuity to the course of events in my life as they relate to the research project.

Life is like money. Stored away, it is worthless. It only has value when used. This brings to mind the archetype of the dragon who hoards his lonely wealth in a dark cave.

The dissertation seems to be coming together. I see a form now, which has been a long time coming, and I feel an out-flowing of gratitude. Guardian spirit?

Devis and devas have multiple aspects or personalities to express their diverse and differing attributes. While they are all-in-one, the human mind is too limited to be able to conceive the combination of pairs of opposites transcended. It is for this reason that we encounter them as separate, even opposed, so as to be able to recognize their attributes in one direction. We see devis and devas with horrifying aspects, because the horrible and terrible are inextricable parts of the whole.

At one point in the Bhagavad Gita, Arjuna asks Krishna to show him his true form. Krishna's like, "You won't be able to handle it." Arjuna asks again. So Krishna shows him his true form, and Arjuna is like, "Ok, Ok! Enough! Go back to your other form!" His limited human mind couldn't handle the totality.

Thursday, 5 May 2016:

"It is the finite that gives meaning to the infinite, because the infinite can only express itself through finite form. And vice versa: where the finite clings to existence for its own sake, without reflecting the infinite, it becomes meaningless and carries the seeds of death within itself. Uniqueness in time and expression is the preciousness of form. It is precious because it is transient as a flower which blossoms and wilts, but which nevertheless expresses the eternal character of all flowers and all life. It is the preciousness of the moment, in which timeless eternity is present. It is the preciousness of individual form, in which the infinite is revealed" (Govinda, 1976).

Friday, 6 May 2016:

This morning, while doing *sadhana*, I felt an uncontrollable trembling and quaking. I felt all wobbly, and I couldn't steady my body. This happened after doing the Kali mantra. She occupied her *murti*, or image, and glowed. Then I was doing the Rudra mantra, and felt the quaking. I am putting more concentrated energy into the *japa*, or mantra repetition. I have the feeling that things would have progressed had I continued on past what is prescribed by my teacher (i.e., more repetitions).

I am coming to understand that this is subjective. These are experiments, and there probably is not one right way of practice for everyone. I've thought of this in relation to prescribed dosages of drugs. Taking the same dose would necessarily have different effects for someone weighing 100 pounds as opposed to someone weighing 200. Yet, for whatever reason, dosages tend to be universal and don't take this into account.

Monday, 9 May 2016:

I feel like I can't do *sadhana* every day. The practice is intense, and I feel like a lot of energy builds up. What to do with all the energy? The days seem so long as it is. The practice has definitely developed. I am unsure what the change has been. Maybe it is that I am surrendering. I understand it better now than I did in the beginning. I understand exerting effort and energy while chanting the mantras, and then absorbing *prana* and Shakti, as I sit in meditation afterwards. I feel my entire body being infused with energy. My mind rests more easily now after intense *japa*.

Watching the breath is strange. It goes on with or without my influence. What is I? I am aware of the breath coming and going, of sometimes influencing it and, at other times it just flowing.

There seems to be something about seeing the practice through fresh eyes, about not stagnating, coming to the practice with new enthusiasm. It seems to help, going off on tangents (which may not really be tangents, but the path itself) and trying different practices, before returning to the same practice again. If an experience happens in meditation, it should not be strived for again. That seems to only create frustration. Other experiences come and go as they will.

There was rain last night. That was a relief. It's been so hot and dry. I can't go out. Though, if it wasn't hot, I'm not sure where I would go.

Tuesday, 10 May 2016:

When *sadhana* goes well, attachment to that fruit arises. The next time I do the practice, I expect the same result. This expectation actually becomes a hindrance to achieving what is expected. I need to be empty and receptive, in a state of surrender, not expecting, not trying to make something happen, but simply letting what happens happen.

Thursday, 12 May 2016:

I didn't do *sadhana* yesterday. The day started off badly, and it escalated. I didn't want to add to the misery with a bad session. Normally, I would have tried to soldier through it. Intuitively, it felt right to pull back. I won't go into all the stupid stuff that went wrong; it could have been anything. Letting go of expectations, of thinking that things need to be a certain way, things improved.

I barely talked in my therapy session. I let the patient talk, and he said several quote-worthy things. It is interesting how much I learn from my patients, how their lives intersect with mine. I am genuinely proud of them and of their effort and progress. They don't know that they have an effect on me.

Around 5:30 in the afternoon, sitting at my home office desk, I felt an earthquake. I was pretty sure that it was an earthquake, but I couldn't find any confirmation on the internet for another hour. This is Mexico. It's kind of strange that others, my wife, didn't notice it. The epicenter was in Jalisco. They are usually in Guerrero. I wonder why I felt this one.

Lying in bed, I felt my third eye (*Ajna*) strongly. Of all the chakras, I always feel this one the most. Maybe looking between the eyebrows stimulates its opening. The point where I look is between the eyebrows, but I feel it in the middle of the forehead. I feel that if I inserted a pin at that spot, I could point to the area in the brain where it is. I had a strange vision there, like an H.R. Giger painting, of a vagina-like opening pretty similar to Hindu images. It was quite vivid.

Sadhana was good today. I did a very active practice, and then sat in meditation.

Sunday, 15 May 2016:

I've been reading through old diaries to see if there is material for my dissertation. I was really crazy shortly after I moved to Mexico. I can hardly recognize the man I was back then. That feels really weird.

Monday, 16 May 2016:

I am getting tired of reading through old diaries. It's a bit depressing and I feel like it's coloring my mood. I am considering just doing a search for Santa Muerte, death, and related words, and being done with it. I don't have to be so thorough. I already have about 100 pages of diary stuff. That's a lot. I probably won't use all of that. I will use the diary to form a time-line, and then I will plot the interviews along that line with appropriate commentary. That should work well.

Thursday, 26 May 2016:

I realize now that, after having had the good idea for the diary-timeline for the dissertation, I got bogged down and depressed (not exactly depressed, but affected) by reading through the old diaries. I should add that the old diaries have yielded little material. I am going to stop reading, and just search for keywords, as I had thought to do before. I will regain the momentum and spare myself the useless nonsense of the past.

Friday, 27 May 2016:

Despite what I said yesterday, I continued through the old diaries. I found some good stuff for the dissertation. I see that I went back to Santa Muerte around the time that I broke up with my wife, then my girlfriend, in 2009. I understand things a little bit better now. I don't feel terrible. I have about sixty pages left, and I am done. I can move on for good.

Monday, 30 May 2016:

Reading all the old diary entries has been painful. Even if the content is not so painful, I hate being dragged back into the past. It's over now, thank God. I culled about 100 pages from around 1000. The parts that I can use range over nine years.

Tuesday, 31 May 2016:

I've been feeling really irritable. The practice of insight (vipassana meditation) had been really good. I could usually remain mindful and in the moment, or bring my mind back to the moment. I didn't mind doing these chores. What happened? I haven't been doing *sadhana*. I haven't been meditating. I know that the answer is there. I need to return, but there is no return. There is just going forward. There is no getting back what is lost. That is the trick. By trying to regain or hold onto things, they make you suffer. That is suffering. The path is winding. I wish that I could learn what is needed without the suffering attached to it.

I feel like I am constantly plugging holes in the dyke. If all around you is in disarray, if your house is not in order, then how can your mind or your life be in order? The worst part is that I have to rely on other people. Whether it's the trash man or my wife, I hate having to depend on or to wait on others. God, I feel so confused!

Thursday, 2 June 2016:

I started looking at weather reports when it got really hot. I realize that I have not looked as much since it started raining and became cooler. This is the same with the i-Ching and other means of divination, I'm only interested in the future when the present is unpleasant. I seek salvation when I'm screwed. I guess the experience of suffering is pretty important to the seeking of the cessation of suffering.

It seems that the things I've been reading lately, all of a spiritual nature, have all put me off; ideologically, they rub me the wrong way. It could be that I come back to these things later with a greater respect. Right now, I am bugged by them.

Monday, 12 September 2016:

"Trust me, the people that I've killed are not people that you would ever want to meet. The world is better without them." The above mentioned Johnny said this to me, and it has kinda haunted me. How can I be sure? Do I simply take the word of a paid killer?

A seasonal ad for Victoria beer. The caption translates as
From Luck and The Skinny One (Death), No One Escapes.

Seasonal packaging of Victoria beer
with Frida Kahlo as a *calavera*

Monday, 10 October 2016:

Back from two weeks in Peru. I wrote in a little notebook that I bought down there. I am very glad to be back. I missed my wife and the cats a lot. However, as I soon as I returned, I had to do tour guide stuff for a colleague from the US and his dad. That was pretty fun.

We ran into Dona Queta at the Tepito shrine. Her husband, Ray, died four months ago. She was in high spirits. I said that I felt sad, that he was a nice man. She corrected me, "*Is* a nice man. He lives forever in here," and she put her hand over her chest, smiling. She was such a ray of light. She was very friendly and welcoming to my guests, Mexicans from the US who don't speak Spanish. She politely told one of them to put away their camera, so as to not invite thieves. I showed her a Santa Muerte tattoo that I had gotten since I saw her last. "How beautiful!" she beamed.

Thursday, 27 October 2016:

When did I become so fearful? When my prayers were answered. When what I had was bad, or when I had nothing, I wasn't afraid. Now that I have good things, I am afraid that they'll be taken away. I was happy when I had nothing.

Wednesday, 2 November 2016:

Last night, a spooky procession, a parade with mariachis, of spooks, paraded down the alley, past our house. My wife was scared. They looked like the undead. Fireworks, as always.

Today, the city was dead. Hardly anyone in the streets. Everything closed. The receptionist at the office I use seemed upset that she had to come in. There were no other doctors or patients. My patients, Westerners, were oblivious to the holiday. I think this is my first Day of the Dead that falls on a weekday. I never remember so much to-do, so much closure.

Thursday, 10 November 2016:

I meant to write this, but didn't for some reason. I had a dream the other night where a figure resembling Sri Mahendranath, the guru of my tantric lineage, (thin, old white man with a long white beard and wearing robes) came to me. He took a pointy razor and made incisions in the centers of my ears, like the Kanaphata Yogis do. The razor looked rusty, but I wasn't afraid. I don't remember much else about the dream. It seems auspicious. The last time I received an e-mail from my guru, Dhruvanath, was 31 August 2015. I don't know what happened. We have never been in constant e-mail contact. Usually, months pass between communications. I've wondered if I angered him somehow. I doubt it. He has always been short on words and high on self-sufficiency. I have wondered if he passed on, but I feel his presence.

Thursday, 29 December 2016:

To have surrendered and then to have been betrayed…this is new for me. I have always had difficulty with surrender. I don't know what happened with my spiritual teacher. I still surrender to the Gods, to Sri Ganesha, to Maha Shakti, and to Sri Shiva. I have left *sadhana* too much. Still, I feel watched over and protected. Things go well without me willing.

I am a bit confused by this, and I am not sure what to say. I enjoy life better with *sadhana* than without. I suppose it would help to have a goal, something to aim for. Anything is possible, as always. Nothing is also possible.

I don't have any great wants or desires. I worry about the future, needlessly. But that silly worry prevents real enjoyment. I guess I feel that I know all there is to know, or that I have experienced all I care to experience.

Silly little things make me happy: fast food (Wendy's, Taco Bell, Taco Bueno, Dunkin' Donuts, Chili's, mostly things that don't exist here), a nice beer, weed that doesn't make me anxious, shopping malls, and suburbs. I know that this sounds crazy. Sometimes I long for ordinary and boring middle-America, where there is order. Sometimes I wish the troglodyte Mexicans with their fireworks at 4am (all hours, any day, really) would all go up in flames. Why are order and reason seen as "oppression"? Doesn't everyone enjoy a nice, quiet time?

Whether the Gods created man or man created the Gods is of little importance. The Gods give meaning to life, and provide a path, a course of action, a way to live, something to aspire to. Don't look to the Gods for reward or punishment. Just try to live as they live, as a creator, as an enjoyer.

Saturday, 28 January 2017:

We never really see ourselves, only reflections. Freud wrote of this as the mirror stage in childhood. That's when the child points to its image in the mirror and says, "That's me!" But it isn't; it's a mere reflection.

To see your true self, you have to go inside. The world is the same. The world you see is a reflection of yourself. In psychology, we typically say *projection*, because it is easier to understand, vis a vis, Hollywood movies. That way we can all understand *projection*. The image projected comes from the projector. We are both the projector and the projected. It is not that hard, then, to make the leap to *reflection*. That the world is your reflection is a little bit more difficult to grasp. It brings the question: Who is reflecting and who is the reflected? Well, it's the same problem as above.

Who is the real image and who the mirror image? Well, they are both images. This is the Lacanian Imaginary. In Lacanian terms, there is the Real, that which is direct experience and before it is filtered through language. Then there is the Symbolic, which it the Real filtered through language, given "expression," and so weakened, as language can never grasp the Real.

Tuesday, 7 March 2017:

I learned that my spiritual teacher, Dhruvanath died suddenly on 28 September 2015 of a brain hemorrhage. I don't know whether I have a preferred way that I would want to die, but that doesn't seem like it.

Saturday, 13 May 2017:

I have to give a warning in my dissertation to future researchers who might trod this path that it is difficult to be so personally involved with the thing. It is fucking depressing to read over old diary entries again and again for years, especially when the subject is death and loss of loved ones.

Tuesday, 10 October 2017:

It's been a long time since I've written here. I went to Costa Rica for two weeks. During that time, there were two big earthquakes in Mexico. The first wasn't too bad for the city, but the second was devastating. I was on the return flight from Costa Rica, when we got an announcement that there had been an earthquake and we were being diverted to Veracruz.

I was full of energy and enthusiasm upon returning to the city, but that steam seems to have evaporated. My computer crapped out. I am typing on a new keyboard that is a bit hard to get used to. One of my patients was in a building that collapsed. He made it out somehow, but 49 others died. Some people were trapped in the rubble for days.

Lots of people have been really freaked out and stressed. My reaction has been: Finally you understand what I've been going through! Because no Mexican has ever understood my PTSD after earthquakes. Now it seems that they get it. Still, the idiots have not changed their behavior. They still sit on stairs, block entries and exits, mill about on the wrong side of the walkway, etc. I thought this would be a learning experience, and that things might change. Nope.

When I returned, I had no trouble getting a taxi from the airport but I had to share with a woman going to Colonia Portales where I used to live. We passed through a blacked-out Iztapalapa. The driver told us to lock our doors and keep the windows up because there were *rateros* about. Things looked ok in Coyoacán. Chedraui was even open. A few things had fallen off the bookshelves, but otherwise ok.

The next morning, I was hurrying to get ready to see a patient. The garden had been neglected while I was gone. There were lots of fallen branches that needed to be cut up for the compost. I was hacking away with the machete, when I brought it down hard on my left-hand finger. I immediately saw that it was deep, dropped the machete, and pressed the thumb of my right hand on the cut. I ran inside, wrapped toilet paper around the finger, and secured it with duct tape. I grabbed a few essentials and went out to the street. I asked a passing lady where I could go for help. She thought a moment, and said that there is a doctor across from Chedraui. It was a Doctor Simi.

The cut was horrible, but I did good first aid. The doctor numbed me, cleaned the wound, and gave me four stitches. I had never had stitches. He charged me about $7US. Later, I looked on the internet to see what the cost would have been in the US. It would cost between $200 and $3000 in the US!!! Crazy!

Freud, working with vets from WWI, found that if a soldier received a physical wound he wouldn't have mental trauma and vice

175

versa. I knew of this. I think I unconsciously gave myself this wound so that I would be spared the mental trauma. It has worked for the most part in these difficult days and weeks after the big quake. I have been able to help others because I know well the PTSD that they are experiencing. I can't help feeling a bit of *Schadenfreude* towards the Mexicans who didn't understand, who called me *puto* for feeling the way I did in the past. Now they know how I felt.

Thursday, 2 November 2017:

Since I hacked my finger with the machete I have been wearing heavy work gloves when I cut up branches. The other morning, I put on a glove and felt a sting. I took off the glove and shook it to get out whatever stung me. Nothing came out. The sting felt like a fire ant, so I thought it might have fallen and I didn't see it. I put the glove back on and did the work I had to do. Near finishing, I felt another sting. I finished up, then I took off the glove and shook it again. Nothing. I filled the glove with water and emptied it. Nothing. I put the glove in the microwave for 30 seconds, and then shook it out. A dead scorpion fell out. I was stung twice by a scorpion!

Nothing much happened. I took some antihistamine. The finger swelled a bit and it hurt, but about like a bee sting. I've been terrified of being stung by a scorpion forever. Now that it's happened, I don't fear them so much. It's a weird string of events, though. I hack my finger with the machete and have to get stitches, so I vow to always use the protective gloves when using the machete. There's a scorpion inside the glove and it stings me on the same finger I hacked with the machete. What irony!

I'm brewing a Belgian Saison ale today. It is day two of Day of the Dead, All Souls Day to Catholics. My wife is off work. There are so many non-working holidays in Mexico. It tires me out, as I am self-employed. Mexicans are much less of a threat when they are occupied with work.

Tuesday, 28 November 2017:

I feel so conflicted. The school has revoked, taken back my pre-approved student loan. It seems that I am not the only one. I was approved for the loan by the government. The school's story is that they have been giving more financial aid than is allowed by the government. It all smells really fishy. So, the school comes up with this 1-unit per quarter (for four quarters) dissertation class for which we have to pay $1000. I think the school is a Chinese intel front, and they want to get rid of the remaining transpersonal people to make way for their drone technology classes.

Now the school is asking me to have transcripts sent from my previous schools and to sign a contract that says I will pay them over $80,000. They say that they have lost my transcripts. I told them that I'm not signing this thing, that I already did all of this in 2011. They act as though they doubt me. But how could I have been accepted into the doctoral program if I hadn't done this stuff? They sent a couple of e-mails warning me that I cannot graduate unless I do this. I feel pressured, and I don't trust these people.

I'm feeling myself in a double bind. I'm afraid I'll be screwed somehow if I sign this thing. I wonder at the value of completing the dissertation, and whether I should just rest at PhD (ABD). If I lived in the US, that might be a bad status. I will never live in the US again. I am not interested in being an academic. Actually practicing psychotherapy has always been my interest. I cannot see any way that a PhD (which I technically already earned) will help or hurt my "career" as a psychotherapist in Mexico. One can practice psychotherapy in Mexico with a bachelor's degree, and I see nothing wrong with that. There are endless, silly obstacles to practice in the US.

I've already paid the school $1000 for this quarter, and I am afraid of my finances being further depleted. I am unsure what to do.

This contract thing looks really shady. I am to agree to pay the fees listed, but in the small print it says that the school can change the fees anytime it wants. It commits me to paying $350 for a graduation I will never attend. It commits me to paying for the school's legal fees should it decide to sue me. And it says that my only legal recourse is through the courts of Santa Clara County, California. I guess the most important part is that it is a contract with "Sofia" University.

I wonder if you know the origin of this name? The perverted scumbag ex-president of the "University," appointed by some nefarious board of directors, came up with this name. He had no idea what transpersonal meant when he came on board. I had lunch with him at a doctoral seminar retreat, and he was noticeably uncomfortable with the transpersonal talk. Right after being made president of the renowned Institute of Transpersonal Psychology, he went to an international transpersonal conference in Sofia, Bulgaria. Coming back to the US, he reported that he was "treated like a rock star." So high was he with his rock star treatment, he decided to rename the Institute of Transpersonal Psychology "Sofia." Then he quickly emptied the school's coffers and disappeared off the face of the earth.

I never agreed to "Sofia." I never signed a contract with this abomination called "Sofia." You say that you lost my transcripts and my contract with the Institute of Transpersonal Psychology. You have threatened me with not graduating. US law specifies that a contract made under duress (i.e., threat) is invalid. So, I am not signing your contract. I do not trust you.

I will give you an analogy. You go out to dinner at an elite restaurant, well known for its exquisite cuisine and the ethical manner by which it obtains its organic produce and by which it kills its free-range stock. This restaurant is renowned for its unique flavors that can be found nowhere else. After being seated, this renowned restaurant reverts to a crappy Chinese restaurant where no one knows whence the food comes. Probably the meat is also secretly dog meat labeled "beef." How would you feel? Would you honor your previous reservation, never mind that you are asked to make a new reservation with the new, changed, dog-meat restaurant. This new school, "Sofia," has lost face. No one respects this school. How much did you pay Depak Chopra, the Oprah Winfrey of Transpersonal Studies, to shill for you? No one is buying it. I'm sure that this is not the point. The school is obviously a front for Chinese intel operations. I don't even care about that. The Chinese can take over the US for all I care. I don't live there.

Thursday, 21 December 2017:

More threatening e-mails from the school. They used many exclamation marks (!!!). "Sign the new contract or else!!!" Like that. They even harassed Jay Dufrechou, my former Chair. I wrote back, saying, "I am tired of your threats! I withdraw!" There are two exclamation marks for them. The chink school president called me today and left a voice message, asking for a favor. Heh! They really are fucked if the dragon lady deigns to speak to a student personally. I guess losing my files will look pretty bad for them while being audited by the Department of Education. Well, they went about all of this the wrong way. I owe them nothing. I hope "Sofia" goes away. ITP was a great thing. "Sofia" is a hungry ghost.

I have a patient who barely escaped a building that fell down in the last earthquake. This building is famous now. It was one of the worst, as 50+ people died there. This was no skyscraper. I think it was five floors. It is miraculous that he got out with a few scrapes. Anyway, he really did die that day. Everything has changed for him. He left his wife. That was a long time coming. Of course, he regrets it in ways now. He's travelling around the world. He feels 'at sea' and he literally is. He is suicidal. "Suicidal" in this sense can be a good thing. He realizes that death is not a thing to be feared as before. He's made a quantum leap in progress, but is suffering greatly for it. As a psychotherapist, I love this. This is exactly what he needed. It is hard, sure, but he will come out much better than before. I know that. Still, I have to be there for him all the time, because I've had to talk him off the ledge more than once. We are going to Oaxaca for Christmas and New Year but I don't get a full-on vacation. I have to remain plugged in, in case he needs me. I'm ok with that. I will be happy to go to Oaxaca City, eat sautéed grasshoppers in corn tortillas with guacamole, go to the mountain cloud forests and eat magic mushrooms, and go to the beach on the Pacific Coast to swim and sunbathe.

Saturday, 23 December 2017:

I think seriously of killing myself every single day. I have since I was a teenager or maybe even before. Something always stops me, though. Curiosity, I guess. I am interested to know how the story will unfold. Really, once you are ready and willing to die, you are completely free.

Thursday, 15 March 2018:

I've felt exhausted since returning from Guatemala. I alternate between near collapsing exhaustion and manic energy. I have so many ideas in my head, so many things that need to be done, and so many possibilities that could be realized.

I am a Psychoanalyst and Psychotherapist. I'm not married to any one theory. I'm influenced by Jung, Freud, Lacan, and Narrative Therapy. As well, I am trained in Transpersonal Psychology. All that aside, one has to live and experience a lot of shit before having the ability to help someone else. I work with the person. It's said often that if your only tool is a hammer, everything starts to look like a nail. Too many people become so married to their theories (usually theories of their betters) that it is amazing that they get anything done at all.

Thursday, 12 April 2018:

One of the positive things about feeling shitty is that I have been writing here every day. I guess one of the reasons that I write, that I have always written, is to write my way out of shitty situations. Writing is very helpful, healing even. This is why I tend to prescribe it to patients.

The weather has been really crazy today. It was cold this morning. Then it became really warm, but cloudy. Then it became cold and really dark and there was a thunderstorm with lots of hard rain and thunder. Then the sun came out and was terribly bright. This is after I had turned on some lamps, as it had been quite dark. Normally, it doesn't rain until June. All of this is weird.

I saw the grotesque Christ image/statue (*El señor de la misericordia*/ The Lord of Mercy) in plaza on the way to the little park and Chedraui supermarket. My old neighbor Don Miguel told me that the people across the street had the image the other day (I thought that was a wake.), and now these other people have it for a time. He told me the legend about the image, which I remembered once he began to tell it.

Some men from Zacatitlan were carrying the image near here, when they stopped at a *cantina* or *pulqueria* to drink. I said, "And when they came out, people from here had stolen the image." "No, no!" Don Miguel said, "They didn't steal it, they found it." I said, "Well, in my culture, if I *lose* something, and you end up having it, you have taken it from me."

He shrugged his shoulders and smiled. The image, which I guess is really old, has been in the possession of this parish for a really long time. I guess they are proud of their gross, bloody Jesus statue. They should add anal rape to the Stations of the Cross! If Jesus had been buggered, more people could relate and then become his slaves. But for me, it's just more drunkenness and thievery, and all the noise and stupidity that goes along with it. Sometimes I hate Mexico.

Sunday, 15 April 2018:

Today has been non-stop *fiesta catolica*. Today, there have been more fireworks than in a long time. That is saying a lot when the fireworks seldom stop around here. Today, they even used some of the kind that produce colorful shapes…but during the day, it's just noise. Fucking idiots. My wife says that they are enemies of beauty. They are used to ugliness, hate beauty, and want to perpetuate ugliness. There were processions of thousands of people moving through the streets and alleyways outside the walls. There were marching bands. And of course, the grizzly image of the crucified Christ. It's all so perverse. This is why I've commented that anal rape should be one of the Stations of the Cross. It's not a great distance from a tortured, bleeding man nailed to a stick with a crown of thorns hammered into his head, to anal rape. It's all so absurd.

Saturday, 9 June 2018:

"Reflect. Why has God been symbolized everywhere as light? Not because God is light, but because man is afraid of darkness.

Man has closed himself completely to darkness. There were historical reasons—because the night was very dangerous, and man was in the caves or in the jungles. In the day he was more secure: he could see all around and no wild animals could attack him; or, he could make some arrangements, some defense—at least he could escape. But in the night everywhere was darkness and he was helpless, so he became afraid—and that fear has gone into the unconscious; still we are afraid.

Your unconsciousness is not your own; it is collective, it is hereditary, it has come down to you. The fear is there, and because of that fear you can have no communion with darkness.

But why are we afraid of darkness? Because light appears to us as life—it is; and darkness appears to be death—it is. Life comes through light, and when you die it appears you have fallen into eternal darkness. That's why we paint death as black, and black has become a color for mourning. God is light, and death is black. But these are our fears projected. Actually, darkness has infinity; light is limited. Darkness seems to be the womb out of which everything falls. If you can love darkness, you will become unafraid of death. Darkness is deathless. Light is born and dies; darkness simply is. It is deathless (Osho, 1972)."

Sunday, 26 August 2018:

"All forms arise out of darkness and dissolve into darkness. Worlds come, are created out of darkness, and they fall back into darkness.

Boundaries exist because of light. When the light is not there, boundaries are dissolved. In blackness nothing is defined, everything merges into every other thing. Form disappears.

That may be one of the causes of our fear—because then you are not defined, then you don't know who you are. The face cannot be seen, the body cannot be known. Everything merges into a formless existence. That may be one of the causes of fear—because you cannot feel your defined existence. Existence become vague and fear enters, because you don't know who you are. The ego cannot exist: undefined, it is difficult to exist as an ego. One feels afraid. One wants light to be there.

Darkness takes away all distinctions. In the light you are beautiful or ugly, rich or poor. The light gives you a personality, a distinctness—educated, uneducated, saint or sinner. The light reveals you as a distinct person; darkness simply accepts you without any definitions. You are enveloped and you become one (Osho, 1972)."

I mentioned previously that the practice of devotion to Santa Muerte is Tantric. Osho was a Tantrika. What he says connects pretty much exactly with what Santa Muerte devotees say.

Conclusion

If this story feels unfinished, that's because it is. I feel that this project is more like an annual report (This one spans over ten years.). It is a representation of what I have learned up to this point. I know that this project never ends, or it ends in death. This book is not a period, but a comma. Perhaps it will spark others to engage with Santa Muerte, with death, and see where things go for them.

Future studies: Throughout this study I found the responses to the questionnaire by the participants to be rather uniform and to yield little interesting content. The questionnaire and the question and answer format are largely to blame. Going into this study, I was not quite sure of the questions I wanted to ask. Beyond that, the format is rather stilted and formal, leaving little room for interesting surprises. I found that meeting participants by chance rather than by active recruitment produced a more vivid picture of what it means to be a devotee of Santa Muerte in Mexico City. Speaking and interacting with a participant over time seems to provide the richest material to the subject.

This is similar to my work with psychotherapeutic patients. Over time, a relationship builds that is much deeper than a cursory question and answer. Because of ethical considerations in the United States, none of my patients were participants in this study. The cultures of the United States and Mexico are very different in many ways. Perhaps a future study could go even deeper with the participation of patient devotees.

Consensus versus interesting: I have never been interested in what is termed consensus reality, that the way the majority sees something is the way that it truly is. The way in which the individual views his or her world is far more real and interesting to me than what a group sees as reality.

During this work I came across a study (Menon & Shweder, 1994) where the researchers patted themselves on the back and called it a day when they could say that x number, the majority, of Indian villagers saw the image of Kali's protruding tongue in the same way. One man that they interviewed saw things very differently. His story they threw out, calling it a "dud." "What lazy idiots!" I thought. But this is the way of the world that privileges quantity over quality, of counting things.

Difficulties recruiting participants: It was not an easy task, going the normal way of recruitment as is done in anthropological or sociological studies (i.e., flyers, web site, etc.). I found that this method was in nearly all cases unacceptable to the population on which the study focuses. Aside from the insular nature of the community, Mexicans tend to preference the spoken word over the written. I found it much easier and more interesting to approach individuals and chat with them to see if there was a chance of doing a proper interview.

My own position as a researcher-devotee was generally found to be important to those with whom I spoke. It is quite likely that had I not been a devotee, the participants would not have trusted me and not wished to participate. The Barrio Tepito community is especially reticent when faced with outsiders.

The personal toll of undertaking such a study: It will likely be obvious from reading the diary excerpts that this was a difficult project for me personally. Though, it is hard for me to see another way that I could have gone about it. I was drawn to the subject emotionally before I was intellectually. For other researcher, some distance from the subject might be helpful in avoiding some of the pitfalls and difficulties that I experienced. However, these difficulties are those of life itself. If a researcher wishes to immerse their self in the subject of investigation, there will necessarily be hardships both physical and mental. To my view, any other approach would yield a much drier and less interesting or revealing outcome.

It is well known from Heisenberg's uncertainty principle and the observer effect that one cannot observe without affecting that which is observed. In 1959, Gregory Bateson and colleagues wrote, "The observer must be included within the focus of observation, and what can be studied is always a relationship or an infinite regress of relationships. Never a "thing."" (Bateson, et al. 1972). The layperson of today generally imagines science to be objective, impartial, and disinterested. Nothing could be further from the truth. The very decision of what to study, which phenomena to observe is already an interested choice on the part of the observer. To pretend that science is not subjective is to mislead.

Appendix:

The Research Problem

At the time of writing this book, very little has been written about Santa Muerte in the English language. Nearly all of my bibliography is written in the Spanish language, and many of the books are anonymous works by devotees. All of my interviews with participant devotees were conducted in Spanish. Where direct translation is necessary, unless otherwise noted, all translations from the Spanish are my own.

There appear to be no research studies involving the psychological experience of devotion to Santa Muerte reported in the psychology literature. This book addresses the need for a qualitative autoethnographic study that seeks to understand, describe, and interpret the individual's experience of practicing devotion to Santa Muerte for me and other devotees in Mexico City, addressing the fact that the practice of devotion to Santa Muerte is little understood and often misunderstood.

In exploring this theme, I do not want to act as a spokesman for a particular way of viewing this phenomenon, but to engage with and discover the various meanings as they converge and diverge for those of us involved with this phenomenon.

Devotion to Santa Muerte is often associated with unsavory elements of Mexican society and with the Mexican drug war. The Roman Catholic Church says that Death is not a saint. Areas explored are: an investigation of Santa Muerte from historical, anthropological, and indigenous perspectives, the practice of devotion, the conflict between the views of Catholic devotees and the Catholic Church, current popular-media associations of devotion to Santa Muerte with the Mexican drug war, and the socioeconomic context for devotion.

A large part of this book is my own diary that I have kept well before and throughout the research and writing of this book. The diary tells the story of my own meeting with Santa Muerte and carries on through the process of research and unveiling of death along the way.

Statement of Purpose

The purpose of this book is to create a qualitative autoethnographic study to understand, describe, and interpret the individual's experience of practicing devotion to Santa Muerte for me and other devotees in Mexico City. The practice of devotion to Santa Muerte is defined as engaging in devotional practices to Santa Muerte that include veneration, prayer, acts, and rituals.

Research Questions

What are the experiences of and the meanings of the practice of devotion to Santa Muerte in the lives of her devotees in Mexico City? Some of the areas of research included are personal devotional practice and how it relates to the larger devotional community, a look at the use of magic and ritual, connections between devotion and transcendence of the fear of death (or death itself), and the implications for the practice of psychotherapy in Mexico City.

Transpersonal Relevance

I first saw Santa Muerte in the form of statues for sale in a market stall (*puesto*) in Mexico City near the Zócalo (which no longer exists) when I first traveled to the city after eulogizing and burying my best friend of twenty-some years in the United States.

I immediately and intuitively understood Her. She spoke to me. She is Death, plain and simple, and she inspires reverence. Seeing Her in this form, venerated by others, I knew that She was kind and that She did not discriminate. I became Her devotee in that moment, if I was not already before.

I was drawn to Transpersonal Psychology, and its approaches to research, because it includes the study of human attraction to manifestations of spiritual power. As stated by Braud and Anderson (1998), transpersonal psychology, "seeks to delve deeply into the most profound aspects of human experience" (p. xxi), including experiences more traditionally studied within the fields of sociology or religion.

I recognized Santa Muerte as what felt like a living force mediating between the phenomenal world of existence (*Becoming*) and the world of spirit (*Being*), or whatever may lie beyond the phenomenal material world. There are few greater transformers than Death, and so I was drawn to the idea that, through research and engagement, "transpersonal researchers learn about the topic and themselves" (p. x).

Research Design

This is qualitative autoethnographic research, looking at the practice of devotion to Santa Muerte in my life and in the lives of devotees in Mexico City. Autoethnography seeks verisimilitude or truth in kind by using thick, rich detail in an artistic presentation of a phenomenon, where the researcher is also a participant. Though criticized by some as lacking the rigor of traditional psychological research, autoethnography has been increasingly used to investigate topics of cultural significance, especially when the author-researcher is also a participant.

In her book *The Ethnographic I,* Carolyn Ellis explains how autoethnography achieves validity: "I look at validity in terms of what happens to readers as well as to research participants and researchers. To me, validity means that our work seeks verisimilitude; it evokes in readers a feeling that the experience described is lifelike, believable, and possible" (Ellis, 2003 p. 124). As I achieve verisimilitude in my research, and as I use autoethnography as the means, then my validity can be documented through the responses of the readers. Ellis continues her explanation of autoethnographic validity: "It helps readers communicate with others different from themselves or offers a way to improve the lives of participants and readers" (Ellis, 2003, p. 124).

Twelve participants for this study were recruited through a process of purposeful sampling (Creswell, 2003) to select those participants best able to help me understand the patterns of the individual's experience of the practice of devotion to Santa Muerte in the lives of her devotees in Mexico City. All participants in the study are devotees in Mexico City without exception.

After willing participant-devotees were located and selected through purposeful sampling, an open-ended interview was conducted and recorded. The content of the interviews was analyzed thematically. I also used observational field notes and reflections collected in a research diary (the main portion of this book is this diary. In fact, if you wish, just skim this academic crap and go right to the diary chapter.), as well as insights gained through dreams and meditation.

Significance of the Study

The originally intended audience of this book were psychologists and other similar professionals, anthropologists, sociologists, et al., but it has branched out, excluding some of the idiotic academic jargon that was used in the dissertation from which this book comes. And I now hope that it will be more accessible and widely read by normal people in Mexico (possibly the rest of Latin America, as the cult spreads) and the United States.

The practice of devotion to Santa Muerte is little understood and often misunderstood. It is often associated with unsavory elements of Mexican society and with the Mexican drug war. While there may be some truth to this, I believe that news media accounts and what little scholarly attention has been given to this phenomenon does not represent its fullness. Since this qualitative autoethnographic study seeks to understand, describe, and interpret the patterns of the individual's experience of practicing devotion to Santa Muerte for me and other devotees in Mexico City, it will be an important contribution to the literature.

This book will also help clinicians who may work with devotees in their practices to understand the phenomenon and to be sensitive to the worldviews of their devotee patients or "clients" (as they say in the US, where business is the model for eveything). The study may be of benefit to politicians and policy-makers in both Mexico and the United States in better understanding the phenomenon and the devotees of Santa Muerte. The study may also help anthropologists and sociologists to see a living picture of the devotees, their lives, beliefs, and practices. And hopefully some of the small-minded prejudice that now exists against Santa Muerte and Her devotees will be transformed into a greater understanding and sympathy.

Organization of the Remainder of the Study

This Introduction chapter will be followed by a Literature Review chapter that will treat the current literature, both scholarly and popular, and a Research Methods chapter that will treat the qualitative autoethnographic and transpersonal paradigms as they apply to this book.

Bibliography

Alvarado Gómez, A. (2004 March, 08). Tradición extranjera: El culto religioso a la Muerte: Resultado de mestizaje [Foreign tradition: The religious cult of death: Result of interbreeding]. México, D.F.: Consejo Nacional para la Cultura y Las Artes. Retrieved from http://paginah.inah.gob.mx:8080/sPrensa/servlets/sSalaPre nsa_04?sFecha=08%20de%20marzo%20de%202004&sTipo _name=nota%20localizada%20el&sTipo2=Noticia&sId=27 22&sTit=TRADICI%D3N%20EXTRANJERA,%20EL%20 CULTO%20RELIGIOSO%20&sSub_tit=Resultado%20del %20mestizaje&sImg_nom=En%20diversas%20partes%20de l%20pa%EDs%20se%20mantiene%20la%20devoci%F3n%2 0a%20la%20muerte&sImg_aut=Archivo%20/%20INAH&s Img_tam=68.6&sFlagCon=1.

Ambrosio, J. (2003). *La Santa Muerte biografía y culto: Ventiseis rituals personales para consequir salud, dinero y amor* [Santa Muerte: Biography and Cult: Twenty-Six Personal Rituals to Obtain Health, Money, and Love]. México, D.F.: Martínez Roca México.

Anderson, R. & Braud, W. (1998). *Transpersonal Research methods for the social sciences: Honoring human experience*. Thousand Oaks, CA: Sage.

Araujo Peña, S. A.; Barbosa Ramírez, M.; Galván Falcón, S.; García Ortiz, A., &Uribe Ordaz, C. (n.d.). El culto a la Santa Muerte: un estudio descriptivo [The cult of Santa Muerte: A descriptive study]. *Revista Psicología*. (México, D.F.: Universidad de Londres). Retrieved from http://www.udlondres.com/revista_psicologia/articulos/sta muerte.htm.

Arriola, A. M. (2003). *La religiosidad popular en la frontera sur de Mexico*

[Popular religiosity on the southern border of Mexico].
México, D.F.: Instituto Nacional de Antropología e Historia.

Bateson, G. (1972). *Steps to an ecology of mind.* New York: Ballantine.

Baez-Jorge, F. (1998). *Entre los naguales y los santos: religion popular y ejercicio clerical en Mexico indigena* [Between Naguales and saints: Popular religion and clerical exercise in indigenous Mexico]. Xalapa, Veracruz, México: Universidad Veracruzana.

Ball, A. (2003). *Encyclopedia of Catholic devotions and practices.* Huntington, IN: Our Sunday Visitor.

Castellanos, L. (2004 May, 9). La Santa de los desesperados [The saint of the desperate]. *La Jornada.* Retrieved from http://www.jornada.unam.mx12004/05/09/mas-santa.html.

Cevallos, D. (2004 January, 30). 'Saint Death' sought for blessings in endless war. *Inter Press Service News Agency.* Retrieved from http://www.ipsnews.net/2004/01/drugs-mexico-saint-death-sought-for-blessing-in-endless-war/.

Chang, H. (2008). *Autoethnography as method.* Walnut Creek, CA: Left Coast Press.

Chestnut, R. A. (2012). *Devoted to death: Santa Muerte, the skeleton saint.* Oxford: Oxford University Press.

Clark, J. M. (1950 July). The dance of death in medieval literature: Some recent theories of its origin. *The Modern Language Review.45*(3), 336-345. Retrieved from http://www.jstor.org/discover/10.2307/3718509?uid=3738 664&uid=2129&uid=2&uid=70&uid=4&sid=476988964504 47.

Creswell, J. W. (2003). *Research design: Qualitative, quantitative, and mixed methods approaches* (2nd Ed.). Thousand Oaks, CA: Sage.

Culto a la Santa Muerte: Incluye novenario [Cult of Santa Muerte: Includes novena]. (n.d.). Ediciones Mercurio.

Daniels, M. (2005). *Shadow, self, spirit: essays in transpersonal psychology.* UK: Imprint Academic.

Dávila, D. (2003 September, 8). Sacrificios satanicos para proteger a narcos. *La Cronica de Hoy.* Retrieved fromhttp://www.cronica.com.mx/nota.php?id_nota=83756.

Diaz del Castillo, B. (1963). *The conquest of New Spain.* J. M. Cohen (Trans.). London: Penguin Books.

Dow, J. W. (1990). *Santos y supervivencias* [Saints and survival]. México, D.F.: Instituto Nacional Indigenista.

Dues, G. (1992). *Catholic customs and traditions: A popular guide.* New London, CT: Twenty-Third Publications.

El culto a la Santísima Muerte, un boom en México [The cult of Santa Muerte, a boom in Mexico]. (n.d.) *Terra.* Retrieved from http://www.terra.com/arte/articulo/html/art9442.htm.

Eliade, M. (1967). *Myths, Dreams and Mysteries* (trans. Philip Mairet), Harper & Row, New York.

Ellis, C. (2003) The ethnographic I: A methodological novel about ethnography. Walnut Creek, CA: AltaMira.

Ellis, C.; Adams, T. E. & Bochner, A. P. (2010). Autoethnography: An Overview [40 paragraphs]. *Forum Qualitative Sozialforschung / Forum: Qualitative Social Research*, 12(1), Art. 10. Retrieved from http://nbn-resolving.de/urn:nbn:de:0114-fqs1101108.

Fernández, A. (1996). *Dioses prehispánicos de México.* Mexico City:

Panorama Editorial.

Ferrer, M. (2008 March, 23). EI culto a la Santa Muerte gana
adeptos en el estado de Jalisco [The cult of Santa Muerte
gains adepts in the state of Jalisco]. *La Jornada Jalisco.*
Retrieved from
http://archivo.lajornadajalisco.com.mx/2008/03/23/index.p
hp?section=politica&article=003n1pol.

Ferriss, S. (2004 March, 9). St. Death calls to the living in Mexico
City. *Atlanta Journal-Constitution.* Retrieved from
http://www.prolades.com/cra/regions/nam/mexico/santa_
muerte_mexico.pdf.

Figueroa, L. (Ed.). (2006). *Altares, ofrendas, oraciones y rituales a la Santa
Muerte* [Altars, offerings, prayers, and rituals to Santa Muerte].
México, D.F.: Ediciones Viman, S.A. de C.V.

Flores Martos, J. A. (2007). La Santisima Muerte en Veracruz,
Mexico: Vidas descarnadas y práicticas encarnadas [Santisima
Muerte in Veracruz, Mexico: Disembodied lives and
embodied practices]. In J. A. Flores Martos, & L. Abad
Gonzáles (Eds.). *Etnografías de   la muerte y las culturas en
America Latina*[Ethnographies of death and cultures in Latin
America](pp. 273-304). Cuenca: Ediciones de la Universidad
de Castilla-La Mancha.

Flores Martos, J. A. (2008). Transformismos y transculturacion de un
culto novomestizo emergente: la Santa Muerte Mexicana
[Transformations and transculturation in an   emerging
Novomestizo cult: Mexican Santa Muerte]. In M. Cornejo,
M. Canton, &, R. Llera, (Eds.) *Teorias y practicas emergentes en
antropología de la religion* [Emergent theories and
practices in anthropology of religion]. *XI Congreso de
Antropología*(pp. 55-76). Logroño: Ankulegi Antropología
Elkartea.

Fragoso Lugo, P. (2007). *La muerte santificada. La fe desde la vulnerabilidad: Devocion y culto a la Santa Muerte en la Ciudad de Mexico* [Sanctified death: Faith from vulnerability: Devotion and the cult of Santa Muerte in Mexico City]. (M.A. thesis). México, D.F.: Centro de Investigaciones y Estudios Superiores en Antropología Social.

Galindo García, A. A. and Galindo Flores, A. E. (2006). *La niña bonita: La Santa Muerte: El culto, trabajos, altares, oraciones, ofrendas, y nuevas recetas/ La niña blanca: La Santa Muerte* [The pretty girl: Santa Muerte: The cult, works, altars, prayers, offerings, and new recipes/The white girl: Santa Muerte]. Chimalhuacan, México: Ediciones Aigam.

Garcia Meza, D. (2008 November, 1). La "Niña blanca" mejor conocida como La Santa Muerte [The White Girl, better known as Santa Muerte]. *El Siglo de Torreon*. Retrieved from http://www.elsiglodetorreon.com.mx/noticia/390200.la-nina-blanca-mejor-conocida-como-la-santa-m.html.

Garma, C. (2009 April, 10). El culto a la Santa Muerte [The cult of Santa Muerte]. *El universal.* Retrieved from http://www.eluniversal.com.mx/notas/590196.html.

Gonzáles Rodríguez, S. (2001 October, 28). La subcultura del narco: La santísima veleidosa [The drug-trafficking subculture: The blessed fickle]. *Reforma.* Retrieved from http://reforma.vlex.com.mx/vid/subcultura-narcosantisima-veleidosa-81393046.

González Olivo, M. (2009). *La biblia de la Santa Muerte* [The bible of Santa Muerte]. México: Editores Méxicanos Unidos.

Govinda, L. A. (1976). *Creative meditation and multi-dimentional consciousness.* Wheaton, IL: Theosophical Publishing House.

Granziera, P. (2004). From Coatlicue to Guadalupe: The image of

196

the great mother in Mexico. *Studies in World Christianity*, 10(2), 250-274.

Gray, S. (2007 October, 16). Santa Muerte: The new god in town. *Time.com*. Retrieved from http://www.time.com/time/nation/article/0,8599,1671984, 00.html.

Graziano, F. (2007). *Cultures of devotion: Folk saints of Spanish America.* Oxford: Oxford University Press.

Griffith, J. S. (2003). *Folk saints of the borderlands: Victims, bandits, and healers.* Tucson: Rio Nuevo Publishers.

Guttman, A. (2007). *Práctica del culto a la Santa Muerte* [Practice of the cult of Santa Muerte]. México, D.F.: Editores Mexicanos Unidos, S.A.

Harden Cooper, R. (2008 February, 14). Vende bien aquí la Santa Muerte [Santa Muerte sells well here]. *El Porvenir.* Retrieved from http://www.elporvenir.com.mx/notas.asp?nota_id=193834.

Holman, E. B. (2007). *The Santisima Muerte: A Mexican folk saint.* Self-published.

Hernández Navarro, L. (2012 May, 15). The tragic consequences of Mexico's failure to tackle organised crime. *The Guardian*. Retrieved from http://www.guardian.co.uk/commentisfree/2012/may/15/t ragic-consequences-mexico-organised-crime

Instituto Nacional de Antropología e Historia. (2008 July, 05). El culto a la Santa Muerte: Rescata la voz de fieles y adversarios [The cult of Santa Muerte: Rescues the voice of the faithful and adversaries]. México, D.F.: Author. Retrieved from http://www.inah.gob.mx/index.php/boletines/247-historia/1015-el-culto-a-la-santa-muerte.

Jimenez, E. (2009 July, 15). La Santa Muerte tendrá su catedral en el DF para 2010 [Santa Muerte will have her cathedral in the federal district in 2010]. *Milenio.* Retrieved from http://www.milenio.com/cdb/doc/noticias2011/0040b737a 39dc5ab49b345a8c196a702.

Johnson, R. (2004 March, 19). A 'Saint' of Last Resort. *Los Angeles Times.* Retrieved from http://articles.latimes.com/2004/mar/19/entertainment/et-johnson19.

Jung, C. G. (1972). *Four archetypes: Mother, rebirth, spirit, trickster.* London: Routledge and Kegan Paul.

Koestenbaum, P. (1971). *The vitality of death: Essays in existential psychology and philosophy.* Westport, CT: Greenwood Publishing Company.

Krause, I. -B. (2003). Learning how to ask in ethnography and psychotherapy. *Anthropology & Medicine, 10*(1), 4-21. doi: 10.1080/1364847032000094487.

Krizek, R. (2003). Ethnography as the Excavation of Personal Narrative. In R.P. Clair (Ed.), *Expressions of ethnography: novel approaches to qualitative methods* (pp. 141–152). New York: SUNY Press.

Lagarriga Attias, I. (1975). *Espiritualizmo trinitario mariano: Nuevas perspectivas de análisis* [Trinitarian Marian spiritualism: New perspectives of analysis].Jalapa, Veracruz, Mexico: Universidad Veracruzana.

Lamas, M. (2002). By Night a street rite: 'Public' women of the night on the streets of Mexico City. In R. Montoya, L. J. Frazier, & J. Hurtig (Eds.), *Gender's Place: Feminist Anthropologies of Latin America* (pp. 238-253). New York: Palgrave MacMillan.

Larios, F. (2012, April 1). Mexican agents probe family in 3 ritual murders. *The Guardian*. Retrieved from http://www.guardian.co.uk/world/feedarticle/10174680.

Los poderosos secretos de la Santa Muerte: Rituales, bálsamos y recetas para el dinero, el amor, y la salud [The powerful secrets of Santa Muerte: Rituals, balms, and recipes for money, love, and health]. (n.d.).

Malvido, E. (2005). Crónicas de la buena muerte a la Santa Muerte en México [Chronicles of   the good death to Santa Muerte in Mexico]. *Arqueología Mexicana, 13*(76), 20-27.

Marmion, Abbot C. (1952, 2005). *Christ, the ideal of the priest.* Dom Matthew Dillon (Trans.) England: Gracewing.

Matos Moctezuma, E. & Solis Olguín, F. (2002). *Aztecs.* London: Royal Academy of Arts.

Matovina, T. & Riebe-Estrella, G. (2002). *Horizons of the sacred: Mexican traditions in US   Catholicism.* New York: Cornell University Press.

Mendelson, M. (1965). *Los escándalos de Maximón: Un estudio sobre la religion y visión del mundo en Santiago Atitlán* [The scandals of Maximón: A study of the religion and worldview in Santiago Atitlán]. Guatemala: Tipografía Nacional de Guatemala, C.A.

Menon, U., & Shweder, R. A. (1994). Kali's tongue: Cultural psychology and the power of shame in Orissa, India. In S. Kitayama & H. R. Markus (Eds.), Emotion and culture: Empirical studies of mutual influence (pp. 241-282). Washington, DC, US: American Psychological Association.

Mertens, D. M. (2005). *Research and evaluation in education and psychology: Integrating diversity with quantitative, qualitative, and mixed methods.* Thousand Oaks, CA: Sage.

Michalik, P. G. (2011). Death with a bonus pack: New age spirituality, folk Catholicism, and the cult of Santa Muerte. *Archives de Sciences Sociales des Religions,* 153(janvier-mars), 159-182.

Miller, M. & Taube, K. (2003). *An illustrated dictionary of the gods and symbols of ancient Mexico and the Maya.* London: Thames & Hudson.

Muir Lovell, C., & Zarur, E. N. C. (2001). *Art and faith in Mexico: The nineteenth-century retablo tradition.* Albuquerque: University of New Mexico Press.

Navarrete Cáceres, C. (1982). *San Pascualito Rey y el culto a la muerte en Chiapas* [San Pascualito Rey and the cult of death in Chiapas]. México, D.F.: Universidad Nacional Autónoma de México: Instituto de Investigaciones Antropológicas.

Ortiz Ehaniz, S. (1990). *Una religiosidad popular: el espiritualismo trinitario mariano* [A popular religiosity: Marian Trinitarian spiritualism]. México, D.F.: Instituto Nacional de Antropología e Historia.

Osho. (1972). *Vigyan Bhairav Tantra Vol. 1.* Retrieved September 27, 2015, from http://www.oshorajneesh.com/download/osho-books/Tantra/Vigyan_Bhairav_Tantra_Volume_1.pdf

Parkinson Zamora, L. (2006). *The inordinate eye: New world baroque and Latin American fiction.* Chicago: University of Chicago Press.

Perdigón Castañeda, J. K. (2008). *La Santa Muerte: Protectora de los hombres* [Santa Muerte: Protector of men]. México, D.F.: Instituto Nacional de Antropología e Historia.

Pérez Arellano, R. (2011 January, 4). *Detienen por secuestro a David Romo, líder de Iglesia de la Santa Muerte* [David Romo detained for kidnapping, leader of the church of Santa Muerte]. *Milenio.* Retrieved from http://www.milenio.com/cdb/doc/noticias2011/1b6bcde8b f538d981ccb8ca58cd480f5

Pieper, J. (2002). *Guatemala's folk saints: Maximon/San Simon, Rey Pascual, Judas, Lucifer, and others,* Albuquerque: Pieper and Associates.

Quezada, N. (1975). *Amor y magia amorosa entre los aztecas: Supervivencia en el Mexico colonial* [Love and love magic among the Aztecs: Survival in colonial Mexico]. México, D.F.: Universidad Nacional Autónoma de México.

Quezada, N. (1989). *Enfermedad y maleficio: el curandero en el México colonial* [Sickness and hex: The *curandero* in colonial Mexico]. México, D.F.: Universidad Nacional Autónoma de México.

Ramirez, M. (2007 September, 30). *Saint death comes to Chicago. Chicago Tribune.* Retrieved from http://www.chicagotribune.com/news/nationworld/death-chicago-08,0,2114588.story.

Read, K. A. & González, J. (2000). *Handbook of Mesoamerican mythology.* Handbooks of world mythology series. Santa Barbara, CA: ABC-CLIO.

Rellea, F. (2008 July, 15). El barrio que venera a la Santa Muerte [The neighborhood that venerates Santa Muerte]. *El Pais.* Retrieved from http://elpais.com/diario/2008/06/15/eps/1213511216_850

215.html.

Santa Muerte: Novena e historia de su culto [Santa Muerte: Novena and history of her cult]. (n.d.). Legaria Ediciones.

Santi, A. (1910). Liturgical Chant. In *The Catholic encyclopedia*. New York: Robert Appleton Company. Retrieved from http://www.newadvent.org/cathen/09304a.htm.

Sevigny, J. (2002 December, 18). In Mexican borderlands, unusual saint of death draws followers. *World Religious News*. Retrieved from http://wwrn.org/articles/9482/.

Smith, M. E., Wharton, J. B., & Olson, J. M. (2003). Aztec feasts, rituals and markets. In T. L. Bray (Ed.), *Archaeology and politics of food and feasting in early states and empires*. New York: Kluwer Academic/Plenum Publishing.

Solucione sus problemas con la Santa Muerte: Manual practico de trabajos: Los poderes mágicos de la Santa Muerte [Solve your problems with Santa Muerte: Practical manual of works: The magical powers of Santa Muerte]. (n.d.). Santa Muerte en Matamoros y Peralvillo, Colonia Morelos, México, D.F.: Ediciones Santa Muerte.

Storey, W. G. (2007). *A Catholic book of hours and other devotions*. Chicago: Loyola Press.

Sunrise, R. (1998). Candle colors and meanings. College Wicca. Retrieved from http://www.collegewicca.com/BOSfiles/candles.html.

Tart, C. T. (1972). States of consciousness and state-specific sciences. *Science*, 176, 1203-1210.

Tertullian. (1999). *Apologeticum (The Apology)*. C. Becker (Ed.). Retrieved

from
http://www.tertullian.org/latin/apologeticum_becker.htm.

Thompson, J. (1998). Santisima Muerte: On the origin and development of a Mexican occult image. *Journal of the Southwest*, 40(Winter). Retrieved from http://findarticles.com/p/articles/mi_hb6474/is_4_40/ai_n 28721107/?tag=content;col1.

Thurston, H. (1911). Popular Devotions. In *The Catholic encyclopedia*. New York: Robert Appleton Company. Retrieved from http://www.newadvent.org/cathen/12275b.htm.

Velázquez, O. (2009). *El libro de la Santa Muerte* [The book of Santa Muerte]. México: Editores Méxicanos Unidos.

Villarreal, H. (2009 April, 5). La guerra santa de la Santa Muerte [The holy war of Santa Muerte]. *Milenio semanal*. Retrieved from http://www.msemanal.com/node/331.

Walker, S. L. (2004 July, 1). Skeleton force: Emerging from shadows on the edge of Mexican society, devotees of Santa Muerte clash with the Catholic Church. *San Diego Union-Tribune*. Retrieved from http://www.utsandiego.com/uniontrib/20040701/news_lz1 c1death.html.

White, M. & Epston, D. (1990). *Narrative means to therapeutic ends*. New York: Norton.

Williams, D. (2011, August 14). *Qualitative inquiry in daily life*. Retrieved May 13, 2014, from http://qualitativeinquirydailylife.wordpress.com/

Woodroffe, J. (2009). *Śhakti and śākta: Essays and addresses on the Śhākta Tantraśāstra*. Leeds: Celephaïs Press.

Yronwode, C. (1995a). Hoodoo in theory and practice. *Luckymojo.com*. Retrieved from http://www.luckymojo.com/young.html.

Yronwode, C. (1995b). Maximón: A.K.A. San Simón of Guatemala. *Luckymojo.com*. Retrieved from http://www.luckymojo.com/maximon.html.

Zarazúa Campa, J. L. (n.d.). *El culto a la* Santa Muerte [The Cult of Santa Muerte]. *Periodismocatólico.com*. Retrieved from http://www.periodismocatolico.com/archivo/b031022/06.htm.

www.ingramcontent.com/pod-product-compliance
Lightning Source LLC
Chambersburg PA
CBHW020254030426
42336CB00010B/752